W9-DHU-115

BODY
THEOLOGY

BY JAMES B. NELSON
PUBLISHED BY THE WESTMINSTER PRESS
The Intimate Connection: Male Sexuality, Masculine Spirituality
Moral Nexus: Ethics of Christian Identity and Community

OTHER BOOKS BY JAMES B. NELSON
The Responsible Christian
Human Medicine: Ethical Perspectives on New Medical Issues
Rediscovering the Person in Medical Care
Embodiment: An Approach to Sexuality and Christian Theology
Between Two Gardens: Reflections on Sexuality
and Religious Experience
Human Medicine: Revised and Expanded Edition
(with Jo Anne Smith Rohricht)

BODY
THEOLOGY

James B. Nelson

Westminster/John Knox Press

Louisville, Kentucky

Scripture quotations are from the New Revised Standard
Version of the Bible, copyright © 1989 by the Division of
Christian Education of the National Council of the
Churches of Christ in the U.S.A., and are used
by permission.

Additional acknowledgment of copyrighted material may
be found at the back of the book.

Book design by
Kristen Dietrich

First edition

Published by Westminster/John Knox Press
Louisville, Kentucky

This book is printed on acid-free paper that meets the
American National Standards Institute Z39.48 standard. ∞

PRINTED IN THE UNITED STATES OF AMERICA

2   4   6   8   9   7   5   3

Library of Congress Cataloging-in-Publication Data

Nelson, James B.
  Body theology / James B. Nelson
      p.   cm.
  Includes bibliographical references.
  ISBN 0-664-25379-2 (alk. paper)

  1. Body, Human—Religious aspects—Christianity.
2. Sex—Religious aspects—Christianity.   I. Title.
BT743.N35   1992   92-3101

For
Josephine B. Nelson
educator, writer, encouraging friend, beloved aunt

Contents

PART FOUR: SERMONIC CONCLUSIONS

Preface

For most of the Christian era we have mistrusted, feared, and discounted our bodies. That remains strangely true in modern cultures such as ours, which frequently glorify and even idolize the body (or at least certain idealized expressions of it). One result of this mistrust is that we have not taken our body experience very seriously in doing our theological reflecting.

Body theology is not primarily a theological description of the body. Nor is it principally an ethical prescription for how we ought to express ourselves physically. Rather, and most simply put, it is doing theology in such a way that we take our body experiences seriously as occasions of revelation. The three foci of this book's essays represent three of my major interests in recent years: sexual theology, men's issues, and biomedical ethics. Each of these three is radically concerned with the body.

Though I may not use the words "sin" and "salvation" very frequently, these realities in body life are the subject matter of this book. Throughout, I assume that wholeness *as bodyselves* is the destiny for which we were created. Further, I assume that, by God's grace, we can realize more of that destined wholeness than we have yet known. But sin is a pervasive reality and is also our continuing experience. Thus, I assume that the dualism that splits us into the war of spirit versus body is a fundamental and enduring problem, not simply a quaint historical note. This alienating dualism manifests itself in a variety of ways. It is clearly present in our sexism and in our homophobia and hetero-sexism. It is present in the distorted and often violent meanings of our cultural masculinity. It is also the basic problem that confuses us in our struggle to use modern medical technologies in the service of human wholeness rather than in its fragmentation. Further, it is a major dynamic that fuels social violence, racism, and ecological abuse.

An incarnational faith boldly proclaims that Christ is alive. In other words, God continues to become embodied in our common flesh in saving, healing, liberating, justice-making ways. To name instances of that experience and to encourage our being open more fully to that possibility are the hopes of this book.

Most of these chapters are revisions of material that I originally prepared for presentation elsewhere. Some have been published previously in somewhat different forms. I here acknowledge with warm thanks the permissions of the following publishers to incorporate revisions of material that I had originally written for them:

- Chapter 1 is based on "Needed: A Continuing Sexual Revolution," copyright 1988 Christian Century Foundation. Reprinted by permission from the June 1, 1988, issue of *The Christian Century*.
- Parts of chapters 2 and 3 are taken by permission from "Body Theology and Human Sexuality," in *Religion and Sexual Health*, ed. Ronald M. Green (Dordrecht: Kluwer Academic Publishers, 1992).
- The early part of chapter 5 is adapted from the Introduction to the British edition of *The Intimate Connection* (London: SPCK, 1991), reprinted with the kind permission of The Society for Promoting Christian Knowledge.
- Chapter 7 includes revised portions of "The Body in Pastoral Counseling," in *The Pastor as Counselor*, ed. Earl E. Shelp and Ronald H. Sunderland (New York: Pilgrim Press, 1991), published here courtesy of The Pilgrim Press.
- A small portion of chapter 8 was originally included in "The Body of Christ and the Human Body: A Different Perspective for Biomedical Issues?" in *Health Care and Its Costs: A Challenge for the Church*, ed. Walter E. Wiest (Lanham, Md.: University Press of America, 1988), and is reprinted by permission.

- Chapter 9 is reprinted by permission from *New Conversations* 13, no. 3 (Summer 1991).
- Portions of chapter 11 were originally published as "What Shapes Us as We Respond to AIDS?" in *AIDS: Ethical Dilemmas of Caring* (Fall 1990), reprinted here by permission of the School of Divinity, University of St. Thomas.

In addition, I want to acknowledge, again with warm thanks, the following organizations and institutions for which I originally prepared much of the remaining material. I have adapted portions of lectures given at conferences at the locations indicated. Naming these occasions brings, in every instance, exceedingly pleasant memories of gracious hospitality and enriching dialogue.

- American Association of Pastoral Counselors (Albuquerque, New Mexico, and Minneapolis, Minnesota)
- Central Union Congregational Church (Honolulu, Hawaii)
- Chautauqua Institution (Chautauqua, New York)
- Claremont School of Theology (Claremont, California)
- Divinity School, Phillips University (Enid, Oklahoma)
- Episcopal Diocese of Newark (Newark, New Jersey)
- Episcopal Divinity School (Cambridge, Massachusetts)
- Institute of Religion, Texas Medical Center (Houston, Texas)
- Kirkridge Retreat Center (Bangor, Pennsylvania)
- Northern California Conference, United Church of Christ (San Francisco, California)
- Planned Parenthood of Kansas City (Kansas City, Missouri)
- Plymouth Congregational Church (Minneapolis, Minnesota)
- School of Medicine, Dalhousie University (Halifax, Nova Scotia)
- Society of Christian Ethics (Los Angeles, California)
- United Church Coalition for Lesbian and Gay Concerns (Cleveland, Ohio)
- United Theological Seminary Chapel (New Brighton, Minnesota)
- World Congress of Sexology (Amsterdam, The Netherlands)

I also want to acknowledge with much gratitude the numerous rewarding explorations of these issues with student and faculty colleagues at United Theological Seminary of the Twin Cities, especially through courses in incarnation and ethics, human sexuality, theology and ethics for men's spirituality, and medical ethics.

Finally and most significantly, I thank Sandra P. Longfellow, M.Div., a former teaching and research assistant who is now a free-lance theological researcher and editor. Sandra graciously assumed the major responsibility for taking twenty-six manuscripts of my lectures, essays, sermons, and articles and shaping them into the present thirteen chapters. In addition, she compiled the index to this volume. Her perceptive insights into the issues, her keen editorial eye, and her collegial spirit have been indispensable in preparing this book for print. I am enormously grateful.

BODY
THEOLOGY

PART ONE

BODY THEOLOGY AND HUMAN SEXUALITY

I

Sexuality and Spirituality: Agenda for a Continuing Revolution

Many people believe that the "sexual revolution" of recent decades is over. Some breathe sighs of relief. Others have regrets. But most agree: it is over. I hope—and I believe—they are wrong.

It is true that our society on the whole has drawn back from some of the excesses in sexual experimentation. It is true that we are reassessing the significance of commitment and, surely in the tragic days of HIV/AIDS, of safer sex. It is true that the voices calling for the return to "traditional family values" have become louder, often more strident. Sadly, it is also true that some of the gains felt by those long sexually oppressed—women, gay men and lesbians, single persons, the aging, persons with disabilities, persons of color—have been imperiled by the backlash.

Some church people have welcomed the backlash. Others of us dare to believe that the old order of patriarchal and heterosexist oppression is beginning to reveal its death throes. We yearn for a new time when the dualism that has made spirit and body enemies of each other will be no more. We yearn for a time when the dualisms that have made men fear and control women, that have made heterosexuals fear and control lesbians and gay men, will be no more. We long for the time when human sexuality, in spite of all its ambiguities, will be more integrated with our experience of the sacred and with the vision of God's shalom.

It is in the spirit of that hope and yearning that I offer these chapters. At the same time, I dare not forget the words attributed to the celebrated English writer Samuel Johnson. Reportedly, he once told an aspiring author, "Your manuscript is both good and original; unfortunately, the parts that are good are not original, and the parts that are original are not good." I am quite aware that in the following pages the insights I believe especially important are not particularly original, for I am gratefully indebted to a "great cloud of witnesses"—many others who share the passion for the reunion of sexuality with a spirituality of justice and celebration. I am also aware that in the insights that may be more particularly mine, I may not be as bold or courageous as I should. Nevertheless, I begin with some reflections on the agenda that lies before us.

Dealing with Urgent Sexual Issues

My first observation should be painfully obvious: the churches simply must deal more forthrightly and creatively with a whole range of urgent sexual issues. While the sexual liberation movements, particularly those of feminist women and lesbians and gay men, have made significant impacts on church and society, the surface of sexual oppression is just being scratched. Organized religion has been, and in some ways still is, the major institution of ideological legitimation for sexual oppression in Western culture. A few examples of our continuing problems are in order.

- The potent combination of sexuality fears and death fears brought together by the HIV/AIDS crisis has almost paralyzed us. We dare not forget that mainline denominations temporized for several years after the epidemic began before initiating any significant responses.
- In society at large and in the pews of our churches there is a genuine hunger for the reunion of sexuality and spirituality, a

hunger still being insufficiently addressed by most theologies that continue to be too rooted in sexual dualisms.

- The eligibility of church members for ordination without regard to sexual orientation continues to be the most divisive issue in many denominations. Indeed, this whole matter often functions symbolically as a carrier of meanings and issues far beyond itself. It is a funnel into which are poured a host of disparate anxieties about authority, about increasing cultural diversity, about perceived threats to personal security.

- Though it appears clear scientifically that sexual orientations are seldom if ever "either-or"—either completely heterosexual or completely homosexual—we are still so rooted in the dualisms of sharply distinguished opposites that we find it almost impossible to deal with the pervasive realities of bisexuality.

- Though the increasing pluralism of marital and family styles is a social fact, churches often find it exceedingly difficult to examine marriage and family critically, fearing that by that very examination we might be weakening already threatened institutions.

- Churches have given too little attention and support to issues of the sexuality of single persons, despite their rapidly growing numbers. Fresh approaches and creative ethics are desperately needed.

- Pornography continues to be a huge, flourishing industry, particularly oppressing women and children, and the churches have not yet discovered how to disentangle healthy erotic sexuality from sexual violence.

- There is an epidemic of teenage pregnancies, and mainline churches intimidated by the religious right have lost nerve about providing sexual leadership for teenagers and being with them in the sexual areas of their lives.

- Sexual abuse and sexual violence are commonplace, underreported, and increasing, and the churches urgently need to break the wall of silence.

- Many clergy deal with their own sexual problems—or do not deal with them. And these clergy issues are finally becoming public.

- The distortions of male sexuality complicate almost every other part of the scene, and the movement for men's change has yet to be vigorously embraced by the churches at large.
- Discrepancies between official church teachings and actual sexual practices of church members raise questions for many about both the church's realism and the church's credibility.

The list of pressing issues could be extended. This situation is, however, not reason for pessimism. Good and important things are happening. I know of no comparable period of time in Christian history when there has been so much open debate and discussion on sexuality issues. I know of no comparable period in which so many sexuality task forces have been appointed, so many conferences held, so many studies and reports written, so many denominational sexual pronouncements given, so many groups organized to change the church or to prevent the church from changing sexually. The ferment is hopeful news. There are more voices speaking and sometimes heard, more indications of movement on sexual issues, than we might have imagined possible not many years ago.

The matter of sexual orientation is a case in point. In a number of mainline denominations, some congregations have declared themselves to be "Open and Affirming Churches," "More Light Churches," "Reconciling Congregations," and the like (the denominational labels vary). These are congregations openly supportive of full lesbian and gay participation. Several years ago, the local congregation of which I am a member was the ordination site of an openly gay man whom we subsequently called to our ministry staff—an event with parallels elsewhere. About the same time our United Church of Christ jurisdiction accepted by a large majority vote a mostly lesbian and gay independent congregation into our denominational fellowship. Several years ago, the General Council of The United Church of Canada officially voted a recommendation to all its ordaining bodies "that sexual orientation in and of itself is not a barrier to participation in all aspects of the life and ministry of the Church, including the order of ministry." On this most divisive and difficult issue of sexual orientation, there is some good news that we dare not forget to celebrate.

However, on this same issue there are also discouragements. If some members are gained, others are often lost when churches take such actions. Currently several major North American Protestant denominations are dramatically wrenched by this matter. The Vatican continues to discipline noted moral theologians for heterodox ethical positions on sexual orientation.

There have been both gains and losses around other sexuality issues. The Christian feminist movement has raised a plethora of fundamental concerns. Despite the resistance, who would deny that in some parts of the church we have seen significant movement regarding women's ordained ministries, inclusive language, reexamination of leadership patterns, rethinking of basic theological imagery, and support of reproductive self-control? And, though her ordination was the occasion for stubborn and sometimes bitter resistance, at last we have a female Episcopal bishop.

Why do the churches still often have difficulty dealing creatively and forthrightly with sexuality in almost any form? Robert Bellah contends that the therapeutic mentality of the liberal middle class renders it uncomfortable with moral argument. Embracing pluralism and the uniqueness of the individual, we conclude that there is no common moral ground and no publicly relevant morality.[1] While I believe this is true, the root problems go deeper and extend much farther back in history than the fairly recent emergence of the therapeutic mentality. They are the continuing power of our inherited sexual dualisms—spirit believed to be essentially different from and superior to body—and its patriarchal counterpart, male believed to be essentially different from and superior to female. The sexual dualisms, though more consciously challenged in recent years, continue to have their formidable grip on our personal lives, on our communal ethos, and on our institutional structures.

Several results can be seen. One is that churches simply shy away from dealing vigorously with sexuality because it seems either incidental or inappropriate to "the life of the spirit." Resistance arises also because serious engagement with virtually any sexuality issue can threaten entrenched male power. Also present is the fear of divisiveness. It is difficult to face sexual issues boldly if we fear that the consequences for the church's

unity and institutional cohesiveness will prove too dire should
we do so. So dualisms, entrenched sexism, timidity, and genuine
concern over the well-being of the church all mingle together.

Another sign of the church's quandary over sexuality is the
fact that we become more reactive than proactive. We focus
attention on our difficulties more than on basic constructive approaches. Like the medical system, we are much more
oriented to the disease than to preventive medicine and health
maintenance.

The combination of our continuing immersion in the sexual
dualisms, a middle-class therapeutic mentality, our fear of division, our reactive tendencies, and the very complexity of sexuality itself all add up to a picture of the church as "an uncertain
trumpet."

Claiming Appropriate Sources and Authority

My second observation is that appropriate sources and authority for sexual theology and ethics continue to be a matter of
struggle. Is scripture a basic and viable source? How about the
church's tradition? For example, what is the usefulness of a
tradition fixated on procreative sex in helping us to sort out
healthy from unhealthy sexuality? Or, regarding sexual violence
and the violation of women, what do we do with so much in
scripture and tradition that is an actual accomplice of these
oppressions? Is a tradition that largely condemns all genital
expression outside heterosexual marriage helpful for an ethic for
single sexuality? How do not only Roman Catholics but others
as well deal with issues of ecclesiology and churchly authority
when the pluralism of Christian conviction on sexual issues butts
up against a church's teaching voice?

The source and authority questions do not end with the
debates about the uses of scripture and tradition. The Wesleyan
heritage argues that there are four interweaving sources of revelation and truth for the Christian: scripture, tradition, reason,
and experience (an approach that I will discuss more fully in
chapter 4). If we are to take that "quadrilateral," or fourfold,
formula seriously (which even a non-Methodist is entitled to do),
we are reminded that reason and experience are vitally important as well as scripture and tradition.

What, for example, of experience? We hear many voices today (some of us, doubtless, are among them) insisting that theology deal more seriously with actual human sexual experience. The voices say we need to listen carefully to women's stories. We need to hear the experiences of those oppressed by sexual violence. We need to hear the gospel speaking profoundly through gay and lesbian experience. We need to hear the voices of those men who are struggling for a richer and more just sexuality. We must listen to teenagers yearning for the church to stand with them. We need to hear the voices of single persons feeling both avoided and condemned by the church in their struggle for responsible sexual expression, and those of disabled persons and the aging, who feel sexually disfranchised by both church and society.

When we take seriously these voices, and our own, we will know the difference between *sexual theology* and the more typical *theology of sexuality*. A theology of (or about) sexuality tends to argue in a one-directional way: What do scripture and tradition say about our sexuality and how it ought to be expressed? What does the church say, what do the rabbis say, what does the pope say? Surely, this question is essential and ought never to be neglected. But it is not enough. We need to ask also (after the manner of various liberation theologies): What does our experience as human sexual beings tell us about how we read the scripture, interpret the tradition, and attempt to live out the meanings of the gospel? The movement must be in both directions, not only in one.

My hope is that out of these struggles in sexual theology, an ethic might increasingly emerge that will have several marks. It will be strongly sex-affirming, understanding sexual pleasure as a moral good rooted in the sacred value of our sensuality and erotic power, and not needing justification by procreative possibility. It will be grounded in respect for our own and others' bodily integrity and will help us defend against the common sexual violations of that integrity. It will celebrate fidelity in our commitments without legalistic prescription as to the precise forms such fidelity must take. It will be an ethic whose principles apply equally and without double standards to persons of both genders, of all colors, ages, bodily conditions, and sexual orientations.

Working on the Content of Sexual Theology

My third observation is that we must continue to work on the central content of a viable sexual theology. Let me illustrate with some more of my own hopes.

A viable sexual theology for our time will affirm that human sexuality is always much more than genital expression. Sexuality expresses the mystery of our creation as those who need to reach out for the physical and spiritual embrace of others. It expresses God's intention that we find our authentic humanness not in isolation but in relationship. It is who we are as bodyselves experiencing the emotional, cognitive, physical, and spiritual need for intimate communion with others, with the natural world, with God.

Such theology will understand our sexuality as intrinsic to the divine-human connection, as one of the great arenas for celebrating the Source of Life. Hence sexuality will enter directly and consciously into our understandings of every major Christian doctrine—God, human nature, sin, salvation, history, and eschatology. For example, we shall need to attend more fully not only to the manifold ways in which our sexuality conditions our perceptions of God (through gendered lenses, for instance), but also to the manifold ways in which the divine-human relationship is permeated with sexual elements, both in our sin and in our salvation. Such theology will understand our sexuality as capable of expressing our intended destiny for freedom, creativity, vulnerability, joy, and shalom. Such sexual theology will express the prophetic critique on every institutional and cultural arrangement that sexually distorts and oppresses; it will be grounded in commitments to equality, justice, and fulfillment.

The ethics that flow from this theology will embrace one standard for evaluating sexual expressions. I believe that standard is love, multidimensional in its reality, with *epithymia* (sexual desire), *eros* (hunger for fulfillment), *philia* (friendship), and *agape* (self-giving) its necessary aspects. No one of those dimensions can be slighted. It is love that is respectful, egalitarian, socially responsible, caring, faithful, honest, and just. Our understanding of such love will be rooted in scripture, tradition, reason, and experience, each source informing, enriching, sometimes correcting the others. Such a central principle of love will welcome numerous presumptive or prima facie rules for guiding our sexual behaviors, but will be wary of specific absolutes that are believed exceptionless and invariant regardless of the context. It will be a single standard, applicable to all persons. Through its acceptance of double standards, unfortunately, the church has done its share of sexually dehumanizing whole groups of persons. Thus, there are many sexual "strangers in the land," consigned to the Egypts of sexual oppression, strangers whom the biblical witness bids be treated with equality and hospitality.

Of particular importance in our time is the reclaiming of the much-neglected, much-feared *erotic* dimensions of love. Fearing that to embrace eros would mean a sanctification of the selfish quest for our own satisfaction, we have too frequently collapsed all meanings of love into agape. We need to recapture a vision of the divine eros as intrinsic to God's energy, God's own passion for connection, and hence also our own yearning for life-giving communion and our hunger for relationships of justice which make such fulfillment possible.

Carter Heyward argues forcefully that the experience of eros is, indeed, the experience of God. While it is true that we fear our erotic power because of our experience of abusive power relations, and such relationships of domination and control have distorted everyone's eroticism in particular ways, the erotic dynamic is still the sacred basis of our ability to participate in mutually empowering relationship—and to know and love God and ourselves.[2]

When we move in this direction we shall embrace a more incarnational theology. Organized religion can learn much here from the witness of lesbians and gays, for when, in the face of social oppression, they affirm themselves they affirm the basic goodness of all human sexuality and of our shared embodiedness. Yet many religious people still learn to fear, despise, trivialize, and be ashamed of their bodies. But if we do not know the gospel of God in our bodies, we may never know it. When we find bodily life an embarrassment to so-called high-minded, spiritualized religion, we lose our capacity for passionate caring and justice, precisely because caring and justice are about embodied creatures. Those of us who are Christians might begin by embracing the scandal of God's continuing incarnation.

All of this means that our images of God need rethinking and expansion. Sallie McFague reminds us that while Christian tradition has insisted that God is love, it has largely recoiled from speaking of God as lover, fearing that "the slightest suggestion of passion in God's love is thought to contaminate it."[3] If the lover relationship is the most intimate of all human relationships, the most powerful and life-giving, might it not be a central metaphor speaking of some aspects of the God-world relationship? When this metaphor is joined with an understanding of the world as God's body, it does not become individualistic and otherworldly but profoundly corporate and holistic. When the "lover" metaphor is used, we might once more reclaim a theology that embraces divine and human pleasure.

Affirming a Continuing Sexual Revolution

My last thematic observation is that we need a continuing sexual revolution. The so-called sexual revolution of the '60s and '70s brought many needed changes, and we ought never to minimize them. It also had its superficialities. On the latter score, there were plenty of pop versions of Wilhelm Reich, maintaining that more and better orgasms were the solution to everything, including world peace. (That formula surely was the dream of every idealistic and horny adolescent.) Even if we recognize some truth in *Time* magazine's cover story one day in April 1984—that by then veterans of the sexual revolution were both bored and wounded—I hope we are at least as troubled by the moral censoriousness of today's fearful, who would return to repression and oppression as the answer.

Beyond our continuing need for more adequate sexual theologies and ethics, numerous specific issues cry out for continuing revolution—ongoing reassessment and change, indeed, metanoia. I have mentioned some of them. There are other issues that also demand our attention if the church as a sexual community is to speak with a credible and helpful voice. Let me suggest a few.

Surely, it is crucial that we continue to join vigorously in the fight against HIV/AIDS and in compassionate ministries to all affected by this scourge. That should go without saying. As the HIV/AIDS crisis worsens, it has the capacity to bring on an antisex hysteria. Beyond anything we have ever known, it has linked in our consciousness the two greatest fears of our society—death and sex. For our synagogues and churches to allow the fear of death to be the major governing agent in our sexual ethics would be an unholy capitulation. We need to help our children to understand and feel good about their sexuality even in a time when sex seems almost synonymous with danger.

What about strong affirmation and support of the sexuality of the aging, the infirm, and those with handicapping conditions? Sadly, religiously sponsored institutions for the care of these folk still all too commonly both deny and punish the sexuality of their residents. Regrettably, clergy routinely ignore the sexuality of such persons in their pastoral care and counseling. The resulting dehumanization is far more serious than most of us realize.

How about sexual rites of passage? Though the synagogue has done somewhat better on this score, aside from the wedding ceremony Christian churches are generally silent about other major sexual occasions of our lives (and the wedding ceremony typically leaves out lesbians and gay men). To the extent that our religious communions are sexually silent, we fail to bring faith's resources of support, guidance, and care to deeply significant aspects of our members' experience. Is it too bold to suggest that we find ways of naming and celebrating the onset of a girl's menstruation? Or the sexual coming of age for boys in the face of the currently destructive secular rituals for naming and achieving "manhood"? Or the affirming of one's sexual orientation? Or the commitment to a new relationship of intimacy other than marriage? Or rites of abortion that convey faith's healing resources after agonized choice? Our congregations are losing countless teenagers and young adults, not to mention older persons, because they continue to be silent, timid, and negative about sexuality.

One of the basic challenges to the church and synagogue, I believe, is to end the sexual hegemony of the nuclear family and the resulting temptation to police the sexuality of everyone who does not fit that mold. Often unwittingly, sometimes intentionally, we have used one narrow family norm in theology, liturgical imagery, religious education materials, and the promotion of family-night suppers. In doing so, we have elevated a relative historical (and bourgeois) social structure to ultimacy, and we have enforced a sexual model that excludes and devalues countless persons.[4]

Correspondingly, we need to rethink the implications of our theologies of marriage. We who are Protestant Christians do well to remember, for example, that it has been more than three hundred years since our spiritual forebears began to understand that God's primary purpose in creating us as sexual beings is not that of procreation, but rather to give us the desire and capacity to love and to bond with others in intimacy. We have generally adopted this conviction as it pertains to heterosexual marriage, but have applied a double standard to those who are same-sex-oriented.

A related agenda item is heterosexism and homophobia. In recent years we have made progress in doing more careful biblical and theological scholarship regarding homosexuality. However, we have hardly begun to deal creatively and vigorously with homophobia and its pervasive institutional and social manifestations in heterosexism. Strongly rooted as it is in male sexism, homophobia not only oppresses gay men and lesbians, it also undermines all male-male relationships, bolsters the ongoing oppression of women, and contributes fearsomely to our social violence.

In the recent "sexual revolution" some were convinced of the truth of a dubious notion that making more love would prevent making war. Nevertheless, there were seeds in that bumper-sticker dictum of a more authentic reality: that our major social ills do, in fact, have profound links to the sexual dualisms that split spirit from body and establish patriarchy. The feminist movement has awakened many of us to the too-long-buried connections between militarism, urban violence, racism, economic exploitation, and ecological abuse, on the one hand, and sexual distortions, on the other hand. The infant movement of a new men's consciousness holds enormous promise in addressing the distorted masculinism that contributes so much violence and peril to our fragile planet.

I am fully convinced that a continuing sexual revolution is an urgent need for the church. I am hopeful but not fully convinced that the churches will engage in that challenge. The ramifications are considerable, and many of them will cause discomfort, at least in the short run. It is no accident, as Charles Curran has observed, that in Roman Catholicism the real *ecclesiological* issues today are being raised especially by those moral theologians working in the area of *sexual* ethics. In part this is true because sexuality is such a significant life dimension which affects everyone personally, and "whenever sexuality and authority meet, a volatile situation is bound to result."[5] It is also true, Curran believes, because of the patriarchal nature of the church and its sexual teachings, its desire to control others, its celibates' fear of sexuality, and its "creeping infallibilism," wherein noninfallible teaching is believed to be certain and absolute.

Though Curran's observations might seem particularly applicable to the Roman Catholic Church, they are relevant to the rest of the churches as well, even those that do not endorse clerical celibacy or infallible teachings. Our continuing patriarchies, our fear of sexuality, our desire to control others—such realities existing throughout the church ought to be reason enough for a continuing sexual revolution. Positively put, the reason is in the gospel: the Word made flesh, and the Word still becoming flesh (Christ is risen!). Doubtless, in many ways "the sexual revolution" of the '60s and '70s is over. Some of the superficial and exploitive forms of "freedom" have proved to be just that. Hurt, boredom, and disease have sobered more than a few. And the forces of religious and political reaction rejoice.

In some other ways, that "mini-revolution" was harbinger of a much more significant change, one that is only just beginning. Is it too bold to call it a paradigmatic shift, a basic shift in the reality model through which we interpret human sexuality? Surely, those words may sound hyperbolic, exaggerated. The shift has not yet taken place. But it is beginning. It is uneven, misunderstood, and resisted, as well as eagerly welcomed and hoped for.

If a shift in sexual paradigm is, indeed, occurring, it will not be the first time in Christian history. There have been others. One occurred when large portions of the church abandoned the notion of the superiority of celibacy over married sexuality. That was a basic shift, and a shift not simply about a particular sexual practice but more deeply about a whole way of viewing sexuality. Another occurred when sizable segments of the church abandoned procreation as the central norm for sexuality. That was another basic shift. Paradigms are never once-and-for-all. In spite of the resistances and obstacles, a new, antidualistic, more incarnational paradigm is now emerging. Martin Buber made a marvelous comment on Søren Kierkegaard's broken engagement, as Robert McAfee Brown reminds us.[6] After long years of courting Regina, the Danish theologian decided that this human love would distract him from the "higher" love of God. So he abandoned her. Buber commented that this was "a sublime misunderstanding of God." Creation, far from being a hurdle on the road to God, is that very road. God draws us to the divine self by means of the Reginas and not by their renunciation. I am struck that in Buber we have one more example of a good, earthy Jew reminding Christians of their calling to a deeply incarnational spirituality. It seems that God, working through another good, earthy Jew two thousand years ago, tried to impress that on us. And still is trying. Apparently, the revolution is not yet over.

2

Where Are We?
Seven Sinful Problems
and Seven Virtuous Possibilities

It is commonly observed that religion is a very ambiguous human enterprise. The creative power of religion is great, for the divine presence is, indeed, often mediated with life-giving power through religious patterns of doctrine, morals, worship, and spirituality. The religious enterprise is also one of the most dangerous of all human enterprises, since it is always tempted to claim ultimate sanction for its humanly constructed beliefs and practices. This ambiguous mix of the creative and the destructive in religion is particularly evident when it comes to religious dealings with human sexuality. That is because the dynamisms of human sexuality give it particular power for both good and ill. Thus, throughout history most religions have given unusual attention to this dimension of human life, have attempted to control it, and often have shown considerable fear of it.

Early in Christian history two lists arose: the seven deadly sins and the seven virtues.[1] The original contents of those early lists are not my concern at this point. I simply want to name seven deadly sins through which the Jewish and Christian traditions have contributed to our sexual alienation, countered by seven virtues or positive resources which these same traditions offer to nurture our sexual wholeness. I am assuming two things. First, the sexual distortions in these traditions have largely resulted from perversions of their own central teachings. Through reclaiming that which is more authentic to the core of these faiths, there may be sexual healing. Second, each of these seven sins betrays profound suspicions of the human body. The body, especially in its sexual dimensions, often evokes anxieties about mortality, loss of control, contamination, uncleanness, personal inadequacy, and a host of other fears. Thus, we sorely need body theologies that will illuminate our experience, and that is a concern of these chapters.

Spiritualistic Dualism or the Bodyself Unity?

Spiritualistic dualism is the first deadly sin. With its counterpart, sexist or patriarchal dualism, spiritualistic dualism underlies and gives shaping power to all the other sins of the list. Any dualism is the radical breaking apart of two elements that essentially belong together, a rupture which sees the two coexisting in uneasy truce or in open warfare.

Though quite foreign to Jewish scriptures and practice, spiritualistic dualism was grounded in Hellenistic Greco-Roman culture and had a profound impact on the early Christian church. Continuing with power to the present, it sees life composed of two antagonistic elements: spirit, which is good and eternal, and flesh or matter, which is temporal, corruptible, and corrupting. The sexual aspects of the body are the particular locus of sin. With this perspective, escape from the snares of bodily life through the spirit's control is central to the religious life.

There is, however, a countervailing virtue in both Judaism and Christianity, one much more authentic to the roots of each faith. In Judaism it is a strong belief in the goodness of creation and with it an anthropology that proclaims the unity and goodness of the human bodyself. The Hebrew scriptures show little reticence about human bodies and their varied functions. Neither do they divide the person into parts or locate the core of personhood in some disembodied spirit. They take for granted the created goodness of sexuality, and at times display lyrical celebrations of the delights of robust, fleshly love.

Christianity also expresses this antidualistic virtue by affirming creation as good, and it adds to this its particular emphasis on divine incarnation. Incarnation proclaims that the most basic and decisive experience of God comes not in abstract doctrine or mystical otherworldly experiences, but *in flesh*. True, the faith's ongoing struggle with dualism has been evident in its marked discomfort over taking incarnation radically. Both Christian doctrine and practical piety have largely confined the incarnation of God to one, and only one, human figure—Jesus of Nazareth. Further, persisting body denial has made most Christians suspect Jesus' full humanity through silence about or actual denial of his sexuality.

There is another possibility, however implausible it may seem to some: without denigrating the significance of God's revelation in Jesus, incarnation might yet be understood more inclusively. Then the fleshly experience of each of us becomes vitally important to our experience of God. Then the fully physical, sweating, lubricating, menstruating, ejaculating, urinating, defecating bodies that we are—in sickness and in health—are the central vehicles of God's embodiment in our experience.

Nevertheless, Christian suspicions of the body and its pleasures continue. The sexual purity campaigns did not end with the Victorian era. But the authentic core of both religious traditions affirm the unity of spirit and body, mind and matter, spirituality and sexuality. The creation-affirming Jewish faith and the incarnational Christian faith attest to the goodness of the bodyself with all its rich sexuality as part of God's invitation into our full humanness and loving communion.

Patriarchal Dualism or Human Equality?

The second deadly sin is sexist or patriarchal dualism. The systematic and systemic subordination of women is the counterpart of spiritualistic dualism, for men typically have defined themselves as essentially spirit or mind, and men have defined women as essentially body and emotion. The logic, of course, is that the higher reality must dominate and control the lower.

Patriarchal dualism pervades Jewish and Christian scriptures and their cultures as well. In Christianity, however, it has taken particular twists that powerfully join the male control of women to body denial. For example, classic understandings of the crucifixion and the atonement have given many Christians throughout the ages the sense that suffering is the necessary path to salvation. At the same time, Christian theology has often denigrated sensual pleasure, suggesting that deprivation and pain are mandatory if eternal joy is to be found. But *women's* suffering has particularly been encouraged, for in patriarchy it is they and not males who essentially represent the evil (the fleshly body) that needs redemption.[2] That sexist dualism is a deadly sin dangerous to the health and well-being of women needs no elaboration. That it is also enormously destructive for males, even while men continue to exercise dominant social power and privilege, needs to be recognized as well.

The *good news,* the countervailing virtue in these religious traditions, is the affirmation of human equality. In one of his better moments the apostle Paul wrote, "There is no longer Jew or Greek, there is no longer slave or free, there is no longer male and female; for all of you are one in Christ Jesus" (Gal. 3:28). The second great wave of feminism in our society, occurring in the latter third of the current century, has produced real gains in gender justice and inclusiveness—few would doubt this. That Jewish and Christian communities have far to go is also beyond question. Continuing resistance to women's religious leadership and ongoing religious justifications for male control of women's bodies are but two of many sad illustrations possible.

Nevertheless, gender equality is a truer expression of our common religious heritage. Sexism is the religious perversion. At the same time, the continuing power of sexist dualism displays a deep fear of the body, and sexism declares that the body is central to woman's being in a way that is not true for the man. All the issues about our bodies are enormously complicated by the interplay of these two faces of dualism, as are all the major moral issues of our day. Not only are the more obvious issues of body rejection, sexism, homophobia, and heterosexism rooted in dualistic dynamics, but so also are crucial dynamics of social violence, militarism, racism, economic oppression, and ecological abuse (about which I shall say more later).

Heterosexism and Homophobia,
or Gay and Lesbian Affirmation?

The third deadly sin is heterosexism (socially enforced compulsory heterosexuality) and its companion phenomenon homophobia (the irrational fear of same-sex feelings and expression). Tragically, this sin has pervaded both Jewish and Christian histories. Yet, it cannot be justified by careful biblical interpretation. The Bible does not even deal with homosexuality as a psychosexual orientation. Such understandings did not arise until the latter part of the nineteenth century. While scriptures do condemn certain homosexual *acts,* they appear to do so because of the lust, rape, idolatry, violation of religious purity obligations, or the pederasty expressed in those acts in specific contexts. We find no explicit biblical guidance on same-sex genital expression in relationships of mutual respect and love. On the other hand, the Bible pointedly celebrates instances of same-sex emotional intimacy, a fact often overlooked by fearful proof-texters.

The dynamics of homophobia are numerous and complex. Frequently they are deeply rooted in misogyny, in the fear of and contempt for the "failed male," in the fear of one's own bisexual capacities, in general erotophobia (the fear of sexuality itself), and in the alienation from one's own body and hence the desperate envy of anyone who appears to be more sexual than oneself.

The good news—the virtue—is that Jews and Christians have significant resources for dealing with these things. The same religious convictions that resist the spiritualistic and sexist dualisms also undercut heterosexism and homophobia. Central to each faith is God's radical affirmation of every person, each unique bodyself. Further, when we experience that grace that pervades the heart of biblical faith, there grows a sense of personal security that releases us from the anxious need to punish those who seem sexually different from ourselves. Then the issue becomes not sexual orientation as such, but rather whether, whatever our orientation, we can express our sexuality in life-giving ways.

That both faith communions are making some progress on issues of sexual orientation seems evident from a number of indications. That this subject is still the most divisive one for many congregations and judicatories is also evident—witness the passionate and often rancorous debate over lesbian and gay ordinations. In all of this one fact seems clear: fear of the body is a central dynamic in the resistance to equality in sexual orientation.

Self-rejection or Self-love?

The fourth deadly sin contributing to sexual dis-ease is guilt over self-love. Christian theologies and pieties have had a more difficult time with this than have Jewish. Dominant Christian interpretations all too frequently have understood self-love as equivalent to egocentrism, selfishness, and narcissism, and hence incompatible with the religious life. A sharp disjunction has been drawn between *agape* (selfless, self-giving love believed normative for the faithful) and *eros* (the desire for fulfillment).

When suspicion about self-love is combined with a suspicion of the body and of sexual feelings, the stage is set for sexual dis-ease. Masturbation is a case in point. To be sure, this subject is no longer inflamed by passions akin to those of the nineteenth-century sexual purity reformers. Sylvester Graham's "graham crackers" and John Kellogg's cornflakes are no longer persuasive as bland diets to prevent the solitary vice, though this was their original purpose. Yet, masturbation is still an obvious arena of guilt, simply because giving oneself sexual pleasure seems to be sheer self-centeredness. *Self-love,* in its larger sense, has had a bad press, particularly in Christianity. And when self-love is denigrated, authentic intimacy with a sexual partner is made more problematic, for true intimacy always is rooted in the solid sense of identity and self-worth of each of the partners.

The good news is that self-love is not a deadly sin. Both Hebrew and Christian scriptures bid us to love our neighbors as ourselves, not *instead of* ourselves. Both religious traditions at their best know that love is indivisible and nonquantifiable. It is not true that the more love we save for ourselves the less we have for others. Authentic self-love is not a grasping selfishness—which actually betrays the lack of self-love. Rather, it is a deep self-acceptance, which comes through the affirmation of one's own graciously given worth and creaturely fineness, our "warts and all."

Furthermore, genuine self-love personalizes the experience of one's own body. "My body *is* me, and I am worthful." When this is our experience, we are less inclined to exploit others sexually or, for that matter, to exploit ourselves. Genuine self-love is essential to our experience of fullest sexual pleasure as well as to an inner-directed sense of sexual responsibility for ourselves and toward others. When we are deeply self-affirming we lose the desire to control others, sexually or otherwise.

Better theological work in recent decades has brought corrections in earlier simplistic condemnations of self-love. Such theological shifts undoubtedly have been undergirded by a growing psychological sophistication within religious communities. Even more important, Christian and Jewish feminists, gay men, and lesbians have shown how dominant males have made the virtue of self-denial a means of controlling those whose sexuality was different from theirs.

Nevertheless, the battle about self-love is far from over, particularly in its sexual expressions. While theological treatises are beginning to give sexual pleasure some justification, most congregations would still be embarrassed by its open endorsement except, perhaps, in a discreet hint spoken during a wedding service. The affirmation of masturbation as a positive good for persons of all ages, partnered or unpartnered, is rarely found in religious writings and even more rarely mentioned aloud in synagogue or church. The sexual and body aspects of self-love surely are not the only dimensions, but they are barometers that remind us how our problems with genuine self-love appear intricately intertwined with our continuing bodily denial.

Legalistic Ethics or Love Ethics?

The fifth deadly sin is a legalistic sexual ethic. Many adherents of both Christian and Jewish faiths have fallen into more legalism about sexual morality than about any other arena of human behavior. Legalism is the attempt to apply precise rules and objective standards to whole classes of actions without regard to their unique contexts or the meanings those acts have to particular persons. Masturbation, homosexual expression, and nonmarital heterosexual intercourse are frequent targets for religio-moral absolutes. So also, however, are numerous issues related to reproduction: contraception, abortion, and various new reproductive technologies such as *in vitro* fertilization.

The virtue that speaks to the deadly sin of legalism is *love*. Our bodyselves are intended to express the language of love. Our sexuality is God's way of calling us into communion with others through our need to reach out, to touch, to embrace—emotionally, intellectually, and physically. Since we have been created with the desire for communion, the positive moral claim upon us is that we become in fact what essentially we are: lovers, in the richest and deepest sense of that good word. A sexual ethic grounded in love need not be devoid of clear values and sturdy guidelines. Indeed, such norms are vitally important. The morality of sexual expression, however, cannot adequately be measured by the physiological contours of certain types of acts. For example, religious legalism typically has condemned genital sex outside of heterosexual marriage and has blessed sex within marriage. Such a morality consequently has prevented us from blessing the loving unions of same-sex couples or finding ways to affirm committed heterosexual relationships short of legal marriage. At the same time, that morality (even if unwittingly) has given moral justification for unloving and exploitive sex *within* marriages by insisting that the rightness of sex is measured not fundamentally by the quality of the relationship but by its external form.

The alternative to sexual legalism is not laxity and license, but an ethic grounded in the centrality of love. Such an ethic is based on the conviction that human sexuality finds its intended and most profound expression in the kind of love that enriches the humanity of persons and expresses faithfulness to God. Such an ethic cannot guarantee freedom from mistakes in the sexual life, but it aims to serve and not to inhibit the maturation and human "becoming" of sexual persons.

Perhaps more than ever, many Christians and Jews are now open to a nonlegalistic approach to sexual ethics. But sexual legalism is not a thing of the past. The unbending stringency of Orthodox Judaism, the official Roman Catholic retreat from Vatican II sexuality teachings, and the strident moralisms of fundamentalist Protestants are still with us. What we seldom recognize, however, is that religious legalism is much more commonly applied to sexuality and body issues than to any other area of human morality. Many people who customarily operate with more flexible and contextually applied rules in other areas of life are wedded to exceptionless absolutes when it comes to sex. That should not surprise us. The body is still a great source of anxiety, and we typically want desperately to control that which we fear.

Sexless Spirituality or Sexual Spirituality?

The sixth deadly sin of which our religious traditions are often guilty is a sexless image of spirituality. This has been a bane of Christianity more than of Judaism, for the church more than the synagogue has been influenced by the Neoplatonic split between spirit and body. In its more extreme forms, such a view perceived true spirituality as sexless, celibacy as meritorious, and bodily mortification and pain as conducive to spiritual purification. In the early centuries of the church, the pressures of the last imperial persecutions brought a new wave of anti-body thought, and an ethic of sexual renunciation took hold in the teachings of the church fathers. Thus, Origen spoke of two distinct creations, the spiritual and the material, one higher and one lower. Acting on his beliefs, Origen actually castrated himself "for the kingdom of God." Similarly, Jerome could say, "Blessed is the man who dashes his genitals against the stone." Tertullian typically connected antisex, anti-body perceptions with a misogynist, anti-woman bias. Speaking to women in one of his sermons, he proclaimed, "The sentence of God on this sex of yours lives on even in our times. . . . You are the one who first plucked the fruit of the forbidden tree; you are the first who deserted the divine law."[3]

While these negative extremes were not the whole story, even in that early period, they dramatically illustrate a significant current that has influenced the Christian sexual story and, unfortunately, still has its hold. In our more recent history it has been "sexual Victorianism." (H. L. Mencken was wrong in his quip about the Puritans. They were not really the ones tortured by the haunting fear that others somewhere else might be enjoying themselves. That was the Victorians—and many others since that time.)

Good news comes in the recognition that a sensuous, body-embracing, sexual spirituality is more authentic to both Jewish and Christian heritages. We are beginning to see that repressed sexuality "keeps the gods at bay" and does not bode well for the fullest, healthiest spirituality. We are beginning to recognize that the kind of erotic and bodily hungers celebrated in the Song of Solomon are human sharings in the passionate longings of God, the divine One who is shamelessly the earth's Lover.

The seventeenth-century Puritan bard John Milton expressed this "delicious Paradise" in his depiction of Adam and Eve beyond the Fall:

> half her swelling breast
> Naked met his under the flowing gold
> Of her loose tresses hid
> . . . .
> Thus these two
> Imparadised in one another's arms
> The happier Eden, shall enjoy their fill
> Of bliss on bliss.[4]

Similarly, incarnational theologians are reclaiming the sacramental possibilities of body experience. Thus Evgenii Lampert described the promise of sexual intercourse:

> It is the mystery of a sudden merging and union into a single indivisible being of flesh and spirit, of heaven and earth, of human and divine love. The divine spirit touches human flesh . . . in the burning moment of erotic ecstasy. We are witnessing to a true *sacrament:* the Spirit of God invades the cosmic element, without ceasing to be Spirit, and the flesh widens into the transcendence of the Spirit, without ceasing to be flesh.[5]

Privatized Sexuality or Personal and Public Sexuality?

The seventh deadly sin of our religions has been the privatization of sexuality. My word play is intentional. Sexuality has been religiously consigned to the nonpublic world and narrowed to a genital matter—"the privates." To that extent, the public, institutional, and justice dimensions of human sexuality have often been neglected.

Yet one of the ironies of American history is that the nineteenth-century "sexual purity movements" most determined to push sex back into the confines and privacy of the marital bed frequently heightened its visibility and made sex a matter of more public discussion. Thus, early in the twentieth century even Anthony Comstock's war on obscenity unwittingly served Margaret Sanger's movement for birth control.[6]

"The personal is public." This familiar feminist affirmation is also a conviction of the Jewish and Christian religious traditions at their best. Sexuality issues are inevitably political, and the most deeply personal is at the same time connected with the social. Yet, there are different ways of understanding this. The radical religious right wing of Christianity exemplifies one. Clearly, sexuality issues are at the core of its public agenda: opposition to gender equality, sex education, abortion, homosexuality, pornography, the Equal Rights Amendment, and family planning, on the one hand, and support of those programs that would strengthen "the traditional family," on the other. Yet, for all its public emphasis on sexuality, the radical right exhibits a thinly veiled fear of it. The two familiar dualisms shape its agenda: patriarchy's hierarchical ordering of the sexes and spiritualism's denigration of the body. The message becomes clear. The right wing's current public sexual agenda is to get sexuality out of the public and back into the private sphere once again. And the private sphere is that of the male-controlled "traditional family."

There is a different way of seeing sexuality as a public issue. It is to recognize that the sharp distinction between private and public is a dualism directly growing out of the sexual dualisms. It is to see that sexual politics is inevitable, for politics (as Aristotle taught us) is the art of creating community, and human sexuality at its core deals with those intimate relationships that shape the larger communities of life. Thus, the bedroom cannot be confined to the bedroom. Justice issues for the sexually oppressed, sexual abuse, reproductive choice, population control, exploitation in commercialized sex, adequate sexuality education—these, among others, are now obviously public issues. Yet, we are only beginning to understand that there are important sexual dimensions to other vast social issues that previously we had not recognized. Social violence is a case in point. Whether it is crime on the city streets, or the arms race, or economic oppression, or the assumptions behind our foreign policies in Vietnam, Central America, or the Persian Gulf, such violence has important sexual dimensions.

To be sure, violence is complex in both causes and manifestations. No single explanation is adequate. But the sexual dimensions of social violence are present, and we have usually overlooked them. What, for example, of the competitiveness, the cult of winning, the armoring of emotions, the tendency to dichotomize reality into either-ors, the abstraction from bodily concreteness, the exaggerated fear of death manifested in a morbid fascination with death? All of these feed social violence, and all of these are deeply related to sexual distortions. Perhaps we are late in recognizing the sexuality embedded in these matters because of our continuing penchant for dualisms. Body anxiety still bids us to keep sex private, or to try to return it to the realm of the private, but it will not be so contained.

So, the seven (or more) deadly sexual sins are still very much with us. Nevertheless, they are neither the last nor the truest word about our religious traditions. I repeat my thesis: While Christianity and Judaism have often confounded good sexuality education and social policies, they have done so through the perversions and distortions of their own central teachings. What is more authentic to the core of both faiths can become the renewed wellspring for sexual health, sexual responsibility, and sexual justice, and for more adequate body theologies.

3

Doing Body Theology

Until recently, most of the Christian and Jewish writings about the body and sexuality were one-directional. They began with religion and moved to the body, not the other way around. They began with such questions as these: What do the scriptures say about our bodily life and how we ought to live it? What does the Vatican say about this or that sexual expression? What does the church teach? The assumption was that religion had its truth, received or arrived at quite independently of our bodily-sexual experience, a truth that then needed only to be applied. Religion provided the instruction book that came with the body appliance, an instruction that often seemed to say "CAUTION: READ CAREFULLY BEFORE OPERATING!"

Remember Søren Kierkegaard's biting comment about his nine-teenth-century contemporary, the German philosopher Hegel. In his monumental, abstract philosophy of religion, Hegel had rationally systematized the human experience of God. Kierkegaard's response was simple and to the point: the philosopher had forgotten only one thing—concrete, particular, existing individuals.

In an analogous manner, our religious tradition has too often forgotten the embodied self. Through the centuries, most theologizing, unfortunately, has not taken seriously the fact that when we reflect theologically we inevitably do so as embodied selves. Male theologians, in particular, have long assumed that the arena of theology is that of spirit and mind, far removed from the inferior, suspect body. Consequently, we have begun more deductively than inductively. We have begun with propositions and attempted to move from the abstract to the concrete. The feminist and the lesbian/gay liberation movements have now reminded us to take body experience as important theological data.

For centuries, however, it was not generally recognized that human bodies are active sources of meaning. Rather, it was believed that bodies were like cameras in a photographic process, simply recording external things mechanistically, things that were passed through the nervous system to form images in the brain according to physical laws. Now, however, there is reason to understand differently.[1] The body has its own ways of knowing. The body often speaks its mind.

Thus, our concern here is not primarily with the "body-object," as studied by the anatomist or physiologist, but rather the "body-subject," the embodiment of our consciousness, our bodily sense of how we are in the world. Our concern is the interaction of the "givenness" of our fleshly realities and the ways in which we interpret them. It is our bodily sense of connections to the world, our bodily sense of the space and time we are in, our bodily knowing of the meanings of our relationships.[2]

Starting with Experience

Body theology begins with the concrete. It does not begin with certain doctrinal formulations, nor with certain portions of a creed, nor with a "problem" in the tradition (though all of these sources may well contribute insight later). Rather, body theology starts with the fleshly experience of life—with our hungers and our passions, our bodily aliveness and deadness, with the smell of coffee, with the homeless and the hungry we see on our streets, with the warm touch of a friend, with bodies violated and torn apart in war, with the scent of a honeysuckle or the soft sting of autumn air on the cheek, with bodies tortured and raped, with the bodyself making love with the beloved and lovemaking with the earth.

The task of body theology is critical reflection on our bodily experience as a fundamental realm of the experience of God. It is not, in the first instance, a theological description of bodily life from a supra-bodily vantage point (as if that were possible, which in actuality it is not). Nor is it primarily concerned with articulating norms for the proper "use" of the body. Body theology necessarily begins with the concreteness of our bodily experience, even while it recognizes that this very concreteness is filtered through the interpretive web of meanings that we have come to attach to our bodily life.

After all, we know the world and respond to it through our embodiedness. That is how as little children we learned to differentiate ourselves from other persons: we touched them, heard their voices, saw their movements as other than our own. As children we learned to make sense of language through body motions and images. If as adults we have been taught to abstract much of our knowledge from the body, that only makes both our knowledge and our bodies less real. Moral knowledge, for example, is bodily: if we cannot somehow feel in the gut the meanings of justice and injustice, of hope and hopelessness, those terms remain abstract and unreal.

The way we feel about our embodiedness significantly conditions the way we feel about the world. Studies in body psychology, for example, disclose strong correlations between self-body connectedness and the capacity for ambiguity tolerance. The more connected and comfortable I am with my bodily reality, the more I am able to accept the confusing mix of things in the world I experience. Contrarily, there are also strong correlations between body alienation and the propensity toward dichotomous reality perceptions: the more I feel distant from my body, the greater my tendency to populate my perceived world with sharply etched "either-ors" (either me or not-me, we or they, good or bad, right or wrong, black or white, sick or well, true or false, heterosexual or homosexual).[3] Our body realities do shape our moral perceptions in ways we have seldom realized.

"We do not just *have* bodies, we *are* bodies." This sentence is both a hopeful statement of faith and a lived experience. It is part of our faith heritage. Hebraic anthropology was remarkably unitary about the bodyself, and when the Christian tradition is purged of its dualistic accretions it too incarnationally proclaims the unitary human being. But let us be clear about the difference between a *dualism* and a *duality*. A dualism (like a dichotomy) is the experience of two utterly different elements at war with each other. At times they may exist in uneasy truce, but always there is hostility. A duality (or polarity) is the perception of two elements which, while distinguishable from each other, truly belong together. Sometimes the two elements may be experienced in creative tension, but always they belong together. Thus, the alienation of body from spirit is dualism, or polarization. The sense that there are different dimensions of myself but that I am essentially one is the perception of duality, or polarity, within my essential unity.

While our self-experience is too frequently dualistic and divisive, we also know the reality of our bodyself unity. That, too, is our lived experience. We feel "most ourselves" when we experience such bodyself integration. When, in illness, the body feels alien to us we say, "I'm not myself today." And we feel most fully ourselves when bodily connected with each other and the earth. The unitary bodyself, then, is not simply an abstract hope, a revelation "from outside" imposed on a very different reality. We are able to articulate this faith claim and we are moved to do so precisely because this too is part of our body experience.

On the other hand, we do live between the times, knowing well the ravages of our body dualisms very personally, but also socially and planetarily. We have been taught that not only is the body different from the real core of selfhood, it is also lower and must be controlled by that which is higher. Our language itself is often strongly dualistic: to say, "I *have* a body" seems much more "natural" than "I *am* a body." Certain experiences— notably illness, aging, and death—seem to confirm the otherness of my body. In those situations, my body seems radically different from me. Though the body is "me," the body is also "it," a thing, a burden to be borne, to be put up with, to be tolerated, sometimes an enemy lived with in warfare or uneasy truce. Then, though the body is "mine," I am also "its."

Thus, for good and for ill, the body has theological and ethical relevance in a host of ways. And our bodily experience is always sexual. Such experience, obviously, is not always genital— actually, only infrequently so. Sexuality is far more than what we do with our genitals. It is our way of being in the world as bodyselves who are gendered biologically and socially, who have varying sexual orientations, who have the capacity for sensuousness, who have the need for intimacy, who have varied and often conflicting feelings about what it means to be bodied. It is all of this body experience that is foundational to our moral agency: our capacities for action and power, our abilities to tolerate ambiguity, our capacities for moral feeling. Our bodily experience significantly colors our interpretations of social relations, communities, and institutions which are the stuff of ethics.

Similarly, our body experience lends considerable shape to our basic theological perspectives. These days we have been frequently and rightly reminded that the images and metaphors we find most meaningful to our experience of God are inevitably connected to our lifelong body experience. In contrast to the anti-body images of experiencing God, listen to the positive body revelation in Brian Wren's hymn "Good Is the Flesh" (based on Gen. 1:31, John 1:14, and John 14:23):

> Good is the flesh that the Word has become,
>   good is the birthing, the milk in the breast,
>   good is the feeding, caressing and rest,
>   good is the body for knowing the world,
> Good is the flesh that the Word has become.
>
> Good is the body for knowing the world,
>   sensing the sunlight, the tug of the ground,
>   feeling, perceiving, within and around,
>   good is the body, from cradle to grave,
> Good is the flesh that the Word has become.
>
> Good is the body, from cradle to grave,
>   growing and ageing, arousing, impaired,
>   happy in clothing, or lovingly bared,
>   good is the pleasure of God in our flesh,
> Good is the flesh that the Word has become.
>
> Good is the pleasure of God in our flesh,
>   longing in all, as in Jesus, to dwell,

glad of embracing, and tasting, and smell,
good is the body, for good and for God,
Good is the flesh that the Word has become.[4]

Interpretive Theory

Even if we are willing to accept our bodyself experience in all its dimensions as relevant and important for our theological-ethical reflections, we are still faced with an important question: By what basic interpretive theory shall we approach this body life? Presently, the two major perspectives are *social constructionism* and *essentialism*. A social constructionist approach emphasizes our active roles as agents, influenced by culture, in structuring our bodily realities. It recognizes that the concepts and categories we use to describe and define our experience vary considerably in their meanings over time and among different cultures and subcultures. Further, it holds that the persistence of a particular interpretation of something depends not only on its correspondence to the reality being described, but at least as much on the usefulness of the concept, often its usefulness in social influence, power, and control.[5]

Symbolic interactionism, as an expression of social constructionism, emphasizes both the highly symbolic world in which we as human beings live and the relatively malleable nature of the realities we experience. Through language, symbols, and gestures we attach meanings to everyday acts and things. We do not respond to the things themselves so much as to the *symbolic meanings* they have for us. And these meanings are always social, arising and being modified and changed through social interaction.[6] For example, the Navahos consider direct eye contact rude and invasive, whereas European Americans believe that avoiding eye contact is evasive, cold, even shifty. The meanings of these bodily gestures are not intrinsically coded into people. They are socially assigned.

Social constructionism can be contrasted with those approaches commonly labeled essentialist or empiricist, which stress the objectively definable reality of topics of investigation. In such a view, the body has its own *intrinsic* meanings. It has a given nature and character, quite apart from what anyone believes about it. Sexuality, for example, may be acted out differently in different times and places, but there is something universal and constant about its core reality. Thus, the official Roman Catholic understanding of natural law assigns to sexual expression an intrinsically procreative meaning. All sexual expressions—such as contraceptive sex, oral sex, anal sex, and masturbation—that deliberately frustrate the procreative possibility are considered unnatural. They are contrary to the created, essential, and intrinsic meaning of genital expression.

Both scientific and popular discussions of sexuality still usually rest on essentialist assumptions. Even though most people reject the notion that contraception is against the natural law and contrary to the essence of sexuality, most still seem to assume that the sexual body is universally the same, always possessing certain sexual drives and needs. Those drives and needs can be socially encouraged or thwarted in various ways and times, but they are fixed in their underlying essential nature.

As with sexuality, so also with issues of bodily health and illness our cultural understandings have leaned strongly toward essentialism. In modern times our bodies have been heavily "medicalized." Using a biomedical model, we give medical meanings to certain bodily conditions or behaviors, defining and classifying them in terms of health and disease. Then authorized medical practice becomes the primary vehicle for eliminating or controlling those conditions or practices defined as diseased or deviant. Such medicalization gives a privileged position to biological discourse and knowledge, assuming that disease and health are objective realities capable of universal definition and standardized practice. When persons with cancer go to Mexico seeking alternative therapies, or when Christian Scientists use prayer for the healing of diseases, most of us assume that these folk (however understandable their intentions) are violating the *essential and objective* truth about the body.

In contrast, a growing minority approach contends that the body is always socially constructed in its particular historical contexts. The body's sexuality, for example, is not so much a "constant"—an essential human quality or inner drive—but rather a human potential for consciousness, behavior, and experience that can be developed and modified by social forces of definition, organization, and control. Thus, it makes sense to say that there are not simply variations of an underlying universal sexuality, there are indeed different sexualities.[7] Regarding health and illness, to be sure, there are given biological realities to most diseases, realities that social interpretations do not, of themselves, create. But what those diseases mean, how they are experienced, how they are treated—such things are never automatically given.

My own approach, while emphasizing social constructionism particularly as shaped by the symbolic interactionists, attempts also to recognize certain claims of the essentialists. Our sexual bodyselves are subject to an enormous range of socially constructed meanings that are extraordinarily plastic and malleable. We need to understand those meanings historically, contextually, and relationally. At the same time, there is still "something there" that is not *simply* the creation of social discourse.

Consider our sexual orientations, for example. Contrary to some recent more extreme constructionist interpretations, I believe that homosexuality is not merely an artifact or construct of particular social structures at particular times and places. There is still something "given" about our sexual orientations, however significant the social meanings that shape their expression. It is also true of our genders. That I have never menstruated but that I do have penile erections does mean *something* for my interpretation of the world. Yet, just *what* these orientations and differently sexed bodies mean is never fixed once and for all. That is hopeful, for if sexual meanings are socially constructed, they can also be reconstructed when they are not life-giving. Indeed, a holistic perception of the bodyself has compelling reasons to hold both constructionist and essentialist perspectives together. Simply put, constructionism alone suggests spirit or mind without bodily reality, and essentialism alone suggests body without spirit.

A relational value theory provides an important framework with which to understand the constructionist-essentialist tension. As H. Richard Niebuhr observed years ago, while most of the value theories in ethics are either objectivist or subjectivist, neither approach is fully satisfactory. The objectivist insists that value actually resides in a particular thing. If I say, "This is a very good table," I am pointing to qualities of worth I believe are actually present in the table, such as its fine construction, design, or beauty. The subjectivist, on the other hand, knows that value simply resides in the feelings and beliefs of the valuer. When I say, "This is a very good table," I know that I am not saying anything objectively real or provable about the table, but rather I am making statements about how I *feel* about it.

Niebuhr, however, suggests that while there is an element of truth in both objectivism and subjectivism, a different interpretation truer to our experience is *relationalism*. While value cannot be simply reduced to our feelings about what we like, neither is value itself an objective kind of reality. Value always arises in relationships, but positive value arises in particular kinds of relationships in which persons, other creatures, or objects connect in ways that complement and fulfill them.[8]

As with values in general, so it is also true with body values in particular. They cannot simply be read off as intrinsic and objective meanings present in bodily life, meanings that are only awaiting our discovery and application. Nor are body values and meanings whatever we feel about them. They neither exist objectively "in" the body, nor are they simply social creations built on a completely plastic, malleable bodily reality. Rather, such meanings and values arise out of the *interaction* of our bodily reality and our interpretive capacities as social, relational beings. Those meanings that contribute to our wholeness as bodyselves in relation are what we deem authentically "valuable."

If body and sexual meanings are always in some measure socially constructed, they can be reconstructed. Descartes, whose philosophy so profoundly influenced the body understandings of modern medicine, taught us that the body is essentially a machine. It is a complex machine, to be sure. But the real person, he believed, "resides" in the mind. "I think, therefore I am." One of the invidious results of this social construction of body meanings is our disconnection from nature. If my body is essentially a complex machine, I am also strongly inclined to view the earth's body mechanistically. I see neither its organic wholeness nor my deep connectedness to it. I feel essentially "other than" the earth. I am not part of it, nor it part of me. The earth and I in our embodiments are machines in proximity to each other—no more.

A reconstruction of the body's meaning, however, is possible. Listen to some far different meanings of the earth and our human bodies. Tradition suggests that Seattle, the Duwamish Indian chief, said this to Isaac Stevens, governor of the Washington Territory:

> Every part of this soil is sacred in the estimation of my people. Every hillside, every valley, every plain and grove has been hallowed by some sad or happy event in days long vanished. The very dust upon which you now stand responds more lovingly to their footsteps than to yours, because it is rich with the blood of our ancestors and our bare feet are conscious of the sympathetic touch.[9]

Similarly, listen to a poet of the earth, Wendell Berry:

> Sowing the seed, my hand is one with the earth.
> Wanting the seed to grow, my mind is one with the light.
> Hoeing the crop, my hands are one with the rain.
> Having cared for the plants, my mind is one with the air.
> Hungry and trusting, my mind is one with the earth.
> Eating the fruit, my body is one with the earth.[10]

Now the body experience is revealing something very different from René Descartes's body-machine. Now it is connection rather than disconnection. Pierre Teilhard de Chardin once commented that we have been taught to understand our bodies as fragments of the universe, as pieces completely detached from the rest, handed over to us to inhabit. We must learn, he said, that the body is the very universality of things. My body is not part of the universe that I possess totally—it is the totality of the universe that I possess partially.[11]

Defining an Incarnational Body Theology

What, then, is body theology? It is nothing more, nothing less than our attempts to reflect on body experience as revelatory of God. How can we understand both the givenness of our body realities and the meanings that we ascribe to them, and how can we interpret these in ways that nurture the greater wholeness of our lives in relation to God, each other, and the earth? Obviously, there is no single path. But one approach of crucial importance to Christians is in exploring the meanings of "incarnation."

Webster's primary definition for incarnation is simply *embodiment*—being made flesh. Theologically, it means *God's* embodiment. Christianly, it means *Christ*. In particular, it means Jesus as the Christ, the expected and anointed one. Through the lens of this paradigmatic embodiment of God, however, Christians can see other incarnations: the *christic* reality expressed in other human beings in their God-bearing relatedness. Indeed, the central purpose of Christology, I take it, is not affirmations about Jesus as the Christ. Rather, affirmations about Jesus are in the service of revealing God's christic presence and activity in the world now.

While this understanding of the main purpose of Christology may seem at odds with much in the tradition, I believe it faithful to tradition's intent. Christologies, our reflections about the meanings of Christ, serve best when they clarify the present activity and embodiment of God, not when they keep our vision fixed on a past epiphany. Indeed, traditional Christologies frequently have raised difficult problems. The formula of a hypostatic union of two natures was largely based on a dualistic metaphysic and has perpetuated it. Beginning with the assumption that divine nature and human nature were essentially foreign to each other, the question then became, how can these two utterly different natures be united in one being?

Confining the divine incarnation exclusively to Jesus has tended to make him a docetic exception to our humanity and has disconnected the christic reality from our experience. Docetism—the early heresy that believed God took on only the *appearance* of human flesh in Jesus, but did not really enter a fully human being—is, unfortunately, still alive and well. Further, focusing on who Jesus was (the divine and human natures) has relegated his actions and relationships to secondary importance. By suggesting to many Christians that belief in a certain Christological formula is necessary for their salvation, such theologies have encouraged Christian triumphalism and have been oppressive to many persons.[12]

I have spoken of essentialism in views of the body and of objectivism in value theory. While I find some truth in each of these, they become distorted, indeed, when taken as the whole truth. Now it is time to name the parallel danger in our views of

Jesus Christ. The danger becomes manifest whenever Christology succumbs to one-sided essentialism and objectivism. This happens when claims are made that through God's unilateral decision and action the "objective" divine essence became embodied in Jesus, quite independently of his own faith, decisions, actions, relationships, and interpretations. When such interpretation holds sway, not only is Jesus' humanity effectively undercut, but also all other human beings are effectively excluded from participation in the christic reality.

What is at stake for body theology is not the paradigmatic importance of God's revelation in Jesus. In our faith community's history, it is this figure and not another who has been and who is central for us. It is through him that we measure the ways we are grasped by the christic presence. But the marvelous paradox is that Jesus empties himself of claims to be the exclusive embodiment of God, and in that self-emptying opens the continuing possibility for all other persons.

The union of God and humanity in Jesus was a moral and personal union—a continuing possibility for all persons. Incarnation is always a miracle of grace, but the essence of miracle is not "interference" in the "natural" world by the "supernatural." It is the gracious (hence miraculous) discovery of who we really are, the communion of divine and human life in flesh. One essential criterion of Christological adequacy must be the moral test. Does this interpretation of Christ result in our bodying forth more of God's reality now? Does it create more justice and peace and joyous fulfillment of creaturely bodily life? Do we experience more of "the resurrection of the body" now—the gracious gift of a fundamental trust in the present bodily reality of God, the Word made flesh?

All this suggests that the human body is language and a fundamental means of communication. We do not just use words. We *are* words. This conviction underlies Christian incarnationalism. In Jesus Christ, God was present in a human being not for the first and only time, but in a radical way that has created a new definition of who we are. In Christ we are redefined as body words of love, and such body life in us is the radical sign of God's love for the world and of the divine immediacy in the world.[13]

This incarnational perspective, only briefly sketched here, is one critical way of beginning to move into the deeper meanings of our body and sexual experience. There are other ways. Yet this path is an important part of the Christian tradition, even if it has often been muted.

It was present, for example, in the later period of the Byzantine Empire, a time in which Christ's transfiguration was seen to be at the very center of our understanding God, ourselves, and the world. It was a time that affirmed that while the final mystery of God will always remain beyond the reach of our faculties, nevertheless, in the energies of the divine action and presence, God is revealed to our bodily senses. This vision of a transfigured world, a vision at the heart of Eastern Orthodoxy, was also present in the Anglican vision of the seventeenth century. In Thomas Traherne's work, for example, it finds remarkable expression: "By the very right of your senses, you enjoy the world. . . . You never enjoy the world aright, till the sea itself floweth in your veins, till you are clothed with the heavens and crowned with the stars, and perceive yourself to be the sole heir of the whole world, and more than so, because others are in it who are everyone sole heirs as well as you."[14]

True, the developments in science and philosophy in the latter days of the seventeenth century muted that theme in the West, and ever since then it has been more difficult to see the bodily consequences of an incarnational faith. The time is upon us for recapturing the feeling for the bodily apprehension of God. When we do so, we will find ourselves not simply making religious pronouncements about the bodily life; we will enter theologically more deeply into this experience, letting it speak of God to us, and of us to God.

The significance of all this has not escaped Toni Morrison in her Pulitzer prize-winning novel, *Beloved*. A central character is Baby Suggs, grandmother and holy woman of the African American extended family who had escaped from slavery in the South only to find continued oppression by the Northern whites. Speaking to her people, Baby Suggs "told them that the only grace they could have was the grace they could imagine. That if they could not see it, they would not have it. 'Here,' she said, 'in this place, we flesh; flesh that weeps, laughs; flesh that dances on bare feet in grass. Love it. Love it hard. Yonder they do not love your flesh. They despise it . . . . You got to love it. You.' "[15] Note carefully Baby Suggs's counsel. The only grace we can have is the grace we can imagine. If we cannot see it, we will not have it.

4

Sources for Body Theology:
Homosexuality as a Test Case

It is no news that matters of sexual orientation for some years now have been the most debated, the most heated, the most divisive issues in American church life. While it is typically an issue approached with fears and passions, it is also susceptible to more understanding than many realize. One church's experience in the mid-'80s speaks to the point.

In Riverside Church in New York City, on May 5, 1985, Dr. Channing E. Phillips, one of the associate ministers, preached a sermon, "On Human Sexuality." Dr. Phillips was an African American minister of considerable national stature in both church and public life. Commenting on words in Genesis 1:27, "male and female [God] created them," he said, "It is difficult to avoid the conclusion that heterosexuality . . . is being lifted up as the model of human sexuality. . . . Those are hard words . . . that imply that deviation from the parable of heterosexual relationship ordained by marriage is contrary to God's will—is sin. . . . And no theological or exegetical sleight of hand can erase that 'word of the Lord.' "[1]

Following the sermon, the sacrament of Communion was celebrated, with Dr. Phillips presiding. After Communion, however, a young straight man from the congregation stood up and walked to the Communion table, interrupting the service. Speaking to the congregation, he stated that he could not support the words from the pulpit that morning. He declared that he would stand by the table during the singing of the last hymn, standing there in support of gay and lesbian people. He invited anyone else who shared his concern to join him. Dr. Phillips said, "I don't mind."

About five hundred of the worshipers, including members of the choir and other clergy staff, left their seats to crowd around the chancel to sing the last hymn together. The *New York Times* would report the event in a prominent story.[2]

The senior ordained clergy team of Riverside Church, "the Collegium," quickly did several things. Part of their approach was to address the matter theologically and with pastoral concern. While for some months they had been in a process of discussing sexual orientation, they invited several theologians to help them consider the issues further.[3] They decided that each of the other three clergy would preach on human sexuality—including homosexuality—on the three following Sundays.

On the next Sunday the senior minister, Dr. William Sloane Coffin, said in his sermon:

> I can only begin to imagine the hurt and anger felt by those of you who thought you had found here at Riverside what you had almost despaired of finding anywhere: a church where, despite the misinformation, superstitions and prejudices of our culture, not only black and white could feel at one and at home, celebrating and affirming each other's existence in the name of Jesus Christ, but also gay and straight. I can also understand the pain of others who thought they had heard confirmed their moral apprehensions about homosexuality . . . only to have these apprehensions then questioned by a demonstration—in church yet! . . . Dearly beloved in the Lord, we now have a sharply divided church, one divided by homosexuality, or should we call it homophobia—the fear of, or contempt for homosexuals. . . . However we label it, it is the most divisive issue the churches of America have encountered, or evaded, since slavery.[4]

Later in his sermon, Coffin made his position clear: "I do not see how Christians can define and then exclude people on the basis of sexual orientation."[5] On the following two Sundays, the other two Collegium clergy, the Rev. Eugene Laubach and the Rev. Patricia de Jong, likewise made clear their convictions affirming the inclusiveness of the church regardless of sexual orientation, and also their pastoral concern for all persons of whatever belief on this issue.

Five months earlier, Riverside Church had begun an intentional process of studying the theology and ethics of sexual orientation. A statement affirming the church's inclusiveness was almost ready for congregational action. Then came Dr. Phillips's dissenting sermon and the demonstration. Immediately the Collegium took additional steps to assure a fair and open process of hearing all viewpoints before the congregational vote was taken. A churchwide retreat on the subject was planned to follow the vote.

Congregational action took place in the weeks following the sermons by each of the Collegium clergy. The vote formally declared Riverside Church to be an "Open and Affirming Church"—fully open to and affirming of lesbian, gay, and bisexual persons. It was the first congregation affiliated with the United Church of Christ to make that formal declaration. This action did not mean that Riverside's struggle was finished. Relationships between many African American and white members had been strained, as was true also between gay and lesbian members and some heterosexual members. The healing process would take considerable time. But the church had faced the issue directly and courageously.

Riverside Church was one of the early congregations, and doubtless the most publicized, to enter this process of reconsidering sexual orientation and church practice in light of the faith. There have been many others. Many issues and questions emerge along the way, issues and questions in addition to the theological-ethical ones. But theological-ethical matters are paramount, and they engage our attention here. How shall we approach them?

Protestants typically have asked, first and foremost, "What does the Bible say?" Roman Catholics typically have asked,

"What does the church say?" Both questions are crucial. Neither is sufficient by itself.

One of John Wesley's legacies is the "quadrilateral" interpretation of authority, an approach with roots in Wesley's own Anglican tradition, and one still used by many persons in many communions. The quadrilateral formula reminds us that when we do our theological reflection, we must draw on more than one source. Wesley himself gave central weight to the scripture. But, over against the biblical literalizers and simplifiers, he argued that scripture must always be interpreted through the Spirit, with the indispensable aid of the church's tradition (which checks our own interpretation against the richness of past witnesses), reason (which guards against narrow and arbitrary interpretations), and experience (which is personal, inward, and enables us to interpret and appropriate the gospel).[6] Let us apply this approach to the subject of homosexuality, surely a test case for the church in our day.

Scripture

A friend of mine, a professor of chemistry at a major university but also by avocation a competent and published theologian, was invited to Washington, D.C., several years ago to give the keynote address to a large convocation of government scientists. The convention's theme was the social responsibility of science. My friend decided to open his speech in a way that would get his audience's attention but also make an important point. Here is what he said:

> I have come to Washington today with a heavy heart, for I am convinced that there are sodomites in high places in government. I am convinced that both houses of Congress have many sodomites in them, the President's cabinet is full of them, and I sadly believe that the President himself regularly practices sodomy. Now I want to tell you what sodomy is. The clearest biblical definition of this sin is not found in the Genesis story but rather in the prophet Ezekiel: "This was the guilt of your sister Sodom: she and her daughters had pride, excess of food, and prosperous ease, but did not aid the poor and needy" [Ezek. 16:49]. That, my friends, is sodomy—it is social injustice, inhospitality to the stranger.

My friend remarked that his opening words did get the audience's attention. And he had made an important point: the real issue, whether for those scientists or for all of us, is justice. By implication, he also made another critical point: the importance of careful interpretation of scripture. The Genesis story of Sodom and Gomorrah, one of the major biblical texts used to condemn homosexuality, was centrally concerned not with sex but with the injustice of inhospitality to the stranger. To the extent that homosexual activity was condemned, it was only homosexual *rape*.[7]

When we approach scripture on the question of homosexual expression, or any other issue, we must always ask two questions.[8] First: What did the text mean? What was the writer trying to say? What questions was the writer addressing? What was the historical context? What literary form was being employed? Answering the question, What did it mean? requires our drawing upon the best insights of biblical scholars with their various forms of critical analysis.

Only after having struggled with the first question, can we proceed to the second: What *does* the text mean *for us today?* Whether a particular text has relevance for us now depends on our answer to two additional questions. First, Is the text consonant with our best understandings of the larger theological-ethical message of the Bible as interpreted through the best insights of the church's long tradition and our reason and experience? Second, Is the situation addressed by the biblical writer genuinely comparable to our own? When, but only when, these criteria are met, the text is ethically compelling for us.

Not many texts in scripture—perhaps seven at most—speak directly about homosexual behavior. We have no evidence of Jesus' teachings on or concern with the issue. The subject, obviously, is not a major scriptural preoccupation. Compare, for example, the incidence of texts on economic justice, of which there are many hundreds. In any event, what conclusions can we reach from careful assessment of the few tests in question?

My own conclusions, relying on the work of a number of contemporary biblical scholars, are several:

We receive no guidance whatsoever about the issue of sexual *orientation*. The issue of "homosexuality"—a psychosexual ori-

entation—simply was not a biblical issue. Indeed, the concept of
sexual orientation did not arise until the mid-nineteenth century.
Certainly, biblical writers knew of homosexual *acts,* but they
apparently understood those acts as being done by heterosexual
people (they assumed *everyone* was heterosexual). Thus, when
persons engaged in same-sex genital behavior, they were depart-
ing from their natural and given orientation. Regardless of our
beliefs about the morality of same-sex expression, it is clear that
our understanding of sexual *orientation* is vastly different from
that of the biblical writers.

It is true, we do find condemnation of homosexual acts when
they violate ancient Hebrew purity and holiness codes. We do
find scriptural condemnation of homosexual prostitution. We
do find condemnation of those homosexual acts which appear to
be expressions of idolatry. We do find condemnation of pederasty, the sexual use of a boy by an adult male for the latter's
gratification.

Note several things at this point. First, scriptural condemnation is also evident for similar *heterosexual* acts—for example,
those that violate holiness codes (intercourse during menstruation), commercial sex, idolatrous heterosexual acts (temple prostitution), and the sexual misuse of minors. Further, the major
questions that concern us in the present debate simply are not
directly addressed in scripture. Those unaddressed issues are the
theological and ethical appraisal of homosexual *orientation,* and
the question of homosexual relations between adults committed
to each other in mutuality and love.

On the other hand, we do find something in scripture that is
frequently overlooked in the current discussions. There are clear
biblical affirmations of deep love between same-sex adults. I am
not implying genital relations in these instances. I simply note
that in the instances of David and Jonathan, Ruth and Naomi,
Jesus and "the beloved disciple," and others, the scripture seems
to hold strong emotional bonding between members of the same
sex to be cause for celebration, not fear.

Robin Scroggs's New Testament scholarship provides an example of the help we need on the biblical question. Looking
closely at the cultural and religious contexts of the relevant New
Testament passages, he discovers that in the Greco-Roman

world there was one basic model of male homosexuality: pederasty, the sexual use of boys by adult males, often in situations of
prostitution and always lacking in mutuality. He concludes that
"what the New Testament was against was the image of homosexuality as pederasty and primarily here its more sordid and dehumanizing dimensions. One would regret it if somebody in the New
Testament had not opposed such dehumanization."[9] In short, the
specific New Testament judgments against homosexual practice
simply are not relevant to today's debate about the validity of
caring, mutual relationships between consenting adults. Nor does
the Bible directly address today's question about the appropriateness of homosexuality as a psychosexual orientation.

However, the problem concerning direct guidance from scripture about specific sexual behaviors is not unique to homosexual
behaviors. The same problem arises with a host of other forms of
sexual expression. The scriptures are multiform and inconsistent
in the sexual *moralities* endorsed therein. At various points there
are endorsements of sexual practices that most of us would now
reject: women as the sexual property of men; the "uncleanness"
of menstrual blood and semen; proscriptions against intercourse
during menstruation and against nudity within the home; the
acceptance of polygamy, levirate marriage, concubinage, and
prostitution. On these matters some would argue that the cultic
laws of the Old Testament are no longer binding, and they must
be distinguished from its moral commandments. Such arguments fail to recognize that most of the sexual mores mentioned
above are treated as moral, not cultic, issues in scripture.

Those Christians who argue that, since Christ is the end of the
law, the Hebraic law is irrelevant, must, if consistent, deal
similarly with New Testament pronouncements about sexual
issues. Even on such a major issue as sexual intercourse between
unmarried consenting adults there is no explicit prohibition in
either Hebrew scripture or the New Testament (which John
Calvin discovered to his consternation). Indeed, the Song of
Solomon celebrates one such relationship. I believe that our best
biblical scholarship reaches Walter Wink's conclusion: "There is
no biblical sex ethic. The Bible knows only a love ethic, which is
constantly being brought to bear on whatever sexual mores are
dominant in any given country, or culture, or period."[10]

This is by no means to suggest that these sources have little to say to us. Consider scripture. As L. William Countryman reminds us, the New Testament frames its particular sexual ethic in terms of purity and property systems that no longer prevail among us. Thus, we cannot simply take numerous New Testament injunctions and assume that they apply literally to significantly different contexts. On the other hand, scripture does for us something far more important. It radically relativizes our theological and ethical systems. It presses toward the transformation—the metanoia, the conversion—of the hearer. It presses us to do our ongoing theological-ethical work in ways that attempt faithfully to discern the inbreaking reign and grace of God in our present contexts. Even if many specific scriptural prescriptions and proscriptions regarding sex are not the gospel's word for today, there are still more basic and utterly crucial scriptural foundations for our sexual ethic.[11]

What are some of those foundations? Surely, they include such affirmations as these: the created goodness of our sexuality and bodily life; the inclusiveness of Christian community, unlimited by purity codes; the equality of women and men; and the service of our sexuality to the reign of God. That incorporation of our sexuality into God's reign means expression in acts shaped by love, justice, equality, fidelity, mutual respect, compassion, and grateful joy. These are criteria that apply regardless of one's orientation. Scripture also offers ample testimony that sexual acts that degrade, demean, and harm others and ourselves are contrary to God's intent and reign. But, for more specific application of such scriptural guidance to issues of homosexuality and same-sex expression, we need to read the scriptures in light of the other three sources.

Tradition

G. K. Chesterton once counseled our taking out "membership in the democracy of the dead." To do so, in Chesterton's thought, is to refuse to submit to that small, arrogant oligarchy of those people whose only virtue is that they happen, at that moment, to be alive and walking about. When we join this democracy of the dead by taking our tradition seriously, we realize that our ancestors in faith and culture have relevant and important insights for us. Truth is not necessarily carried by the book with the latest copyright date.

However, the postbiblical tradition provides no more un-ambiguous guidance on specific sexual expressions than does scripture. Selective literalism in use of the tradition is almost as common as it is in the use of scripture itself. Most of us would fully endorse the tradition's movement toward monogamy and fidelity. Many of us would endorse the tradition's growth to-ward the centrality of love as the governing sexual norm. Many of us would celebrate those parts of the tradition that not only tolerate but positively affirm gays and lesbians, including lesbian and gay clergy. But few of us would endorse those elements of tradition which baptize patriarchal oppression, endorse violence against women, oppress lesbians and gays, exalt perpetual vir-ginity as the superior state, or declare that heterosexual rape is a lesser sin than masturbation (since the latter is a sin against nature while the former, while also sinful, is an act in accordance with nature). As with scripture, it is impossible to find one consistent, coherent sexual ethic in the postbiblical tradition.

Of what use, then, is the long sweep of Christian tradition regarding homosexual orientation and expression? On this sub-ject, I believe that tradition most helpfully poses a series of questions—challenges to much of our conventional Christian wisdom.

One question is this: Has the church's condemnation of gay and lesbian people been consistent throughout its history? As Yale historian John Boswell has demonstrated, a careful exami-nation of tradition yields a negative answer. Indeed, for its first two centuries, the early church did not generally oppose homo-sexual behavior as such. Further, the opposition that did arise during the third to sixth centuries was not principally theologi-cal. Rather, it was based largely on the demise of urban culture, the increased government regulation of personal morality, and general churchly pressures toward asceticism. Following this period of opposition, however, ecclesiastical hostility to homo-sexuality largely disappeared once again. For some centuries there was no particular Christian antagonism toward homosex-uality, and legal prohibitions were rare. Indeed, the eleventh-century urban revival saw a resurgence of gay-lesbian literature and leadership in both secular society and the church. Once again, though, hostility appeared late in the twelfth century— now as part of the general intolerance of minority groups and their presumed association with religious heresies.

Our conventional wisdom has assumed that Christian history has been all of one piece, uniform in its clear disapproval of homosexuality. In fact, a closer look at the tradition tells us that there were periods of remarkable acceptance. Further, we are reminded to interpret the theological opposition that was, indeed, often present in the context of broader changes occurring in the surrounding society.

Another challenge to us, suggested by the tradition, is this: Has the church always agreed that heterosexual marriage is the appropriate sexual pattern? The answer is no. Singleness, particularly celibacy, was prized above marriage for much of the time from the church's beginnings to the sixteenth-century Reformation. Moreover, a careful look at tradition reveals that heterosexual marriage was not celebrated by Christian wedding services in church worship until perhaps the ninth century. We have no evidence of Christian wedding rites until that time. Obviously, many Christians married during these earlier centuries, but marriage was considered a civil order and not a rite of the church. Curiously, there is some emerging evidence that unions of gay or lesbian Christians were celebrated in some Christian churches earlier than heterosexual marriages. All of this suggests that heterosexual marriage has not always been central as the norm for Christian sexuality.

The tradition suggests a third question: Is it true that procreation has always been deemed primary to the meaning and expression of Christian sexuality? That is, if we do not use our sexuality with the intent to procreate or at least with the possibility of doing so, is there something deficient about it? It is an important question, for the procreative norm has often been used to judge lesbians and gays adversely: "Your sexuality is unfit to bless because your acts are inherently nonprocreative."

Once again, tradition casts large question marks on many current assumptions. In those times wherein celibacy was more highly honored than marriage, it is obvious that procreative sex was not the norm—it was second class on the ladder of virtue.

But what of the centuries, particularly since the Reformation, when marriage has been blessed as the normative Christian calling?

Still the answer is no. In the seventeenth century, a number of Christians—especially among the Puritans, Anglicans, and Quakers—began to teach, preach, and write about a new understanding. It appeared to them that God's fundamental purpose in creating us as sexual beings was not that we might make babies, but that we might make love. It was love, intimacy, mutuality, not procreation, that were central to the divine intention for sexuality. Some Puritans, for example, declared that if children were born to a marriage, that was "an added blessing," but not the central purpose of the marriage.

The centrality of love, companionship, and mutual pleasure in the meaning of sexuality has been embraced by most Protestants during the last three hundred years and, in practice, by numerous Catholics, even if not with Vatican approval. The proof in heterosexual relations is the use of contraception as a decision of conscience. Most of us do not believe we must be open to procreation each time we make love—in fact, we believe strongly to the contrary. The curious double standard still exists, however; the procreative norm has been smuggled in the back door and applied negatively to lesbians and gay men.

Thus, while the church's tradition may not give definitive answers to specific questions about homosexual orientation and same-sex expression, it raises questions—these and others—that challenge conventional wisdom and refocus our perspectives.

Reason

In searching for God's truth, theologically and ethically, we need to draw on the best fruits of human reason, a third source from the quadrilateral. Wesley put it this way: "It is a fundamental principle with us that to renounce reason is to renounce religion, that religion and reason go hand in hand, and that all irrational religion is false religion."[12]

One of the ways we honor our God-given reason is in striving for consistency and adequacy in our theological judgments. These two age-old tests of the philosophers are perennially relevant. Consistency eschews the use of double standards. Adequacy prods us to judgments that do justice to the widest range of data.

Reason is also expressed in the various sciences, our disciplined human attempts to understand creation. Biological, psychological, and social sciences can shed significant light on questions of sexual orientation. What, for example, might we learn?

In 1948 Alfred Kinsey and his associates jarred America with the first major study of the sexual behaviors of persons in this society. In his volume on the male, he presented two things that particularly caught the public eye regarding sexual orientation. One was the continuum on which orientations might be represented. Challenging either-or assumptions (one is *either* homosexual *or* heterosexual), Kinsey introduced evidence suggesting that we might be "both/and." The other finding, widely reported in the press, was Kinsey's discovery that at least 50 percent of the male population had experienced homosexual genital relations at some time in their lives, and for 37 percent of them it was orgasmic behavior after puberty. This alone startled many, simply because it appeared to be evidence that same-sex attraction and expression were not just the province of a tiny minority.[13]

Though most of us tend toward one or the other side, it is probable that the vast majority of us are not exclusively either heterosexual or homosexual. Kinsey's conclusions were substantiated by his studies on the American female five years later and by subsequent research by others. Indeed, in recent decades, most sexologists have not only validated Kinsey's continuum but have also added other dimensions to it. While Kinsey was primarily interested in behaviors (genital experiences culminating in orgasm), later sexologists have argued that when other dimensions of orientation—such as fantasy, desire, social attraction, or emotional preference—are added to the picture, it is probable that none of us is exclusively one or the other. Most of us have more bisexual capacities than we have realized or than we have been taught in a bifurcating society. This recognition is of particular importance when we come to try to understand some of the dynamics of homophobia.

Another question on which the sciences shed some light is the origin of sexual orientation. While there is still much debate, at least two things seem clear. One is that our orientations are given, not freely chosen. The likelihood is that they arise from a combination of genetic and hormonal factors, together with environmental and learning factors—both nature and nurture. The other general agreement is that our sexual orientations are established rather early in life, most likely somewhere between the ages of two and five, and thereafter are largely resistant to any dramatic changes. "Therapies" that attempt to change persons from homosexual to heterosexual are now discredited by reputable scientists. Such procedures may change certain behaviors, they may make some people celibate, but they will not change deep feelings and most likely will produce great psychic and emotional confusion. These facts, too, are relevant to the theological-ethical questions.

Further, stereotypes about gay men and lesbians wither under scientific scrutiny. For example, the notion that homosexual males are more likely to abuse children sexually than are heterosexual males has been thoroughly disproved. Linking emotional instability or immaturity with homosexuality, likewise, is no longer scientifically tenable. Granted, lesbians and gay men suffer emotional distress from their social oppression, but this is far different from assuming that the cause of this distress lies in their orientation.

These issues do not exhaust, but simply illustrate, the ways in which the uses of human reason, including the human sciences, provide important insights for our theological reflection and understanding of scripture.

Experience

The fourth and last area of insight comes from experience. Wesley was rightly suspicious of trusting all the vagaries of human experience. Experience by itself is not reliable, nor does it give a consistent picture. However, without the validation of scriptural insight by experience as well as reason and tradition, such insight remains abstract and uncompelling. The Spirit, Wesley believed, inwardly validates God's truth through our experience. I believe that is true. And I also believe that we must expand the focus of "experience" to include the careful examination of both individual and common experience to find those things which nurture wholeness and those things which are destructive to our best humanity.

Our experience of *homophobia,* in careful examination, provides one key example. The term refers to deep and irrational fears of same-sex attraction and expression or, in the case of lesbians and gay men, internalized self-rejection. Though the word was coined only within recent decades, the reality has long been with us.[14] Another term, *heterosexism,* more recently has come into use. It too is helpful, for it reminds us that prejudice against gays and lesbians is not simply a private psychological dynamic but, like racism and sexism, is also structured deeply into our institutions and cultural patterns. While I clearly recognize the pervasive realities of heterosexism, in this illustration of the uses of experience in doing body theology I will focus on homophobia.[15]

I lived the first forty years of my life assuming that I was completely heterosexual. That had been my sexual experience, and that was my only awareness. Then, through some volunteer work in urban ministries I came into close interaction, for the first time that I consciously recognized, with a number of articulate gay men and lesbians. They challenged my stereotypes and my homophobia, and they launched me into a process of examining my own experience.

One thing I discovered was that homophobia was a particularly acute problem for males—it certainly was for me. For the first time I realized that my fear of lesbians and gays was connected to issues in my own masculine identity. Gay males seemed to have an ill-defined masculinity, a threat to any man in a society where one's masculinity seems never achieved once and for all and always needs proving. Lesbians threatened my masculinity simply because they were living proof that at least some women did not need a man to validate or complete them as persons.

Gay males were a problem for me also, I realized, because they threatened to "womanize" me (a threat to any male in a sexist society where men have higher status). The gay could treat me simply as a sexual object, a desirable body—not a full person. I had to admit that this was the way that men (myself included?) had treated so many women for so many years. Now the tables were turned.

Examining my experience made me aware, further, that I might be involved in what the psychologists call reaction formation and projection. If it is true that all of us are a mix of heterosexual and homosexual capacities (even though we happen to be considerably more of one than the other), and if it is true that we have been taught by a rigidly bifurcating society to deny the existence of anything homosexual, what do we do with any same-sex feelings that might arise? We vigorously defend against them in ourselves by projecting them onto others and blaming those others for having more obviously what we, to some extent, may also experience. Though I had not been conscious of same-sex desires, I needed also to examine this possibility in my experience, for some capacity was likely there.

Another factor I discovered was simply sexual envy. Looking at gays and lesbians through stereotypical lenses, I had been seeing them as very sexual people. That, in part, is what stereotyping does to the stereotyper—it gives us tunnel vision. I did not see them fundamentally as persons with richly multifaceted lives; I saw them fundamentally and almost exclusively as sexual actors. The result was obvious: they appeared more sexual than I. And this was a cause for envy, particularly to a male who has been taught that virility is a key sign of authentic masculinity.

Still another contribution to my homophobia, I discovered, was intimacy envy. As a typical man, I had difficulty making close, deep, emotionally vulnerable friendships, especially with other men. Yet, deep within, I sensed that I yearned for such friendships. Then I saw gay men closely bonding with each other, apparently having something in friendship that I too wanted—male-to-male emotional intimacy. I was pressed to look at my experience again, this time to see if my intimacy envy and consequent resentment were part of my homophobia.

Further, confronting my own fears meant confronting my fears of sexuality as such—my erotophobia. Though I had long enjoyed the sexual experience, I came to realize that, reared in a dualistic culture, I was more distanced from my sexuality than I cared to admit. Reared as a male and conditioned to repress most bodily feelings, reared as "a good soldier" and taught to armor myself against any emotional or physical vulnerability, I discovered I was more alienated from my body than I had acknowledged. Gay males and lesbians brought into some kind of dim awareness my own erotophobia because they represented sexuality in a fuller way.

The fear of death may sound like a strange contributor to homophobia, but it is likely there. Though in Christian community we are named people of the resurrection, our reassurances in the face of mortality are often grounded much more by children and grandchildren. The thought of childless persons awakens fear of death. And while many gays and lesbians have produced and parented children, they stand as a key symbol of nonprocreating people. In this way also, I realized, they caused me fear, but once again it was fear of myself.

Homophobia thrives on dualisms of disincarnation and abstraction that divide people from their bodily feelings and divide reality into two opposing camps. As never before we need gracious theologies. Homophobia thrives on theologies of works-justification, wherein all persons must prove their worth and all males must prove their manhood. As never before we need erotic theologies. Homophobia thrives on erotophobia, the deep fear of sexuality and pleasure. Homophobia thrives in eros-deprived people because it grows in the resentments, projections, and anger of those whose own hungers are not met. As never before we need theologies of hope and resurrection. Homophobia thrives wherever there is fear of death, for then people try to dominate and control others to assure themselves of their own future. Homophobia thrives on bodily deadness, so deeply linked as it is with sexual fear and repression. Though its varied dynamics are complex, the root cause of homophobia is always fear, and the gospel has resources for dealing with fear.

These are a few of the dynamics of homophobia that I became conscious of in my own experience some years ago. Doubtless, there are others. I have focused particularly on the male experience both because that is my own and because I believe homophobia is a particularly severe problem for dominantly heterosexual males such as I. Nevertheless, it is a disease that affects all of us—female as well as male; lesbian, gay, and bisexual as well as heterosexual. Homophobia is an example of the experience that enters into our theological and ethical reflection on issues of sexual orientation (and many other matters as well). Our awareness of these dynamics in ourselves gives us heightened self-critical consciousness, an important ingredient of theological-ethical reflection.

I have not attempted here to present a fully developed theological-ethical perspective on sexual orientation. My attempt is far more limited. It has been to name and to illustrate some uses of the four major sources of interpretation—scripture, tradition, reason, and experience—so important to the churches' responses to the most troubling and divisive question facing them.

My own bias is evident. Just as homophobic fears are not principally about "them," but about myself and about us all, so also the basic issue is not homosexuality but rather *human* sexuality. Our sexuality, I believe, is a precious gift from God, critically important as part of a divine invitation. It is an invitation that we come together with each other and with God in relationships of intimacy and celebration, of faithfulness and tenderness, of love and justice. Our sexuality is a gift to be integrated fully and joyously into our spirituality. Our orientations, whatever they may be, are part of that gift—to be received with thanksgiving and honored by each other.[16]

PART TWO

SOME
MALE
ISSUES
IN
BODY
THEOLOGY

5

Men and Body Life:
Aging as a Case Study

In a moment of exasperation Sigmund Freud once asked, "What do women *want*?" Now we are asking, "What do men want?" When I have asked that question—of myself as well as of other men—the answers form a predictable litany:

"I want close friendships—especially with other men."

"I want to know women as equals and as real persons."

"I want to work without always feeling I have to prove myself."

"I want to reconnect with my father, even though he is dead."

"I want to know my children in a way I haven't before."

"I want to understand what I'm feeling. I might even want to cry sometimes."

"I want to be able to play without having to win."

"I want to live without expecting to die seven years earlier than women."

"I want to live in a world without so much male violence."

"I want a deeper spirituality."

"I want to feel good about being a man again."

For at least the past twenty-five years, feminists have reminded us that the institutions, the language, and the thought
patterns of Western culture and religion disproportionately reflect the dominant male experience. Men, however, usually had
assumed that these meanings were not specifically male but
simply human. "Man" and "mankind," we thought, meant all
of us. In more recent decades we have learned that such language
and assumptions invariably do injustice to women, and also to
those men marginalized by the dominant males, particularly
gays and men of color.

Though our consciousness of this assumption is now much
higher, what we have failed to notice is that treating dominant
males as generically and normatively "human" has made men
largely invisible to themselves. It has prevented men from self-
consciously and self-critically exploring their own distinctively
masculine experience. Now, for a variety of reasons, we are
motivated as never before to inquire what our masculinity really
means, what it means to have a male body, and what the
particular hungers, joys, pains, and satisfactions of a man's life
are.

The Emergence of a Men's Movement

It started in the early 1970s. Men began coming together in
small consciousness-raising and support groups. The feminist
movement was the initial spur. For one thing, men saw women
gathering to tell their stories, to laugh and cry together, to
experience a special bonding. Observing this, numerous men
realized that they wanted and needed a similar experience.
Another reason, however, was simply the havoc that some men
were feeling as a result of the women's movement. Their familiar
worlds had become unsettled and confusing. Even though gender roles were oppressive to men as well as to women, the
familiarity of those patterns carried a certain kind of comfort.
Now everything once nailed down appeared to be coming loose.

Men's support groups have continued to multiply in the past
two decades. Some would say that there is now "a men's movement." If by movement one means that there is a clear and
reasonably unified doctrine emerging, that is not the case. But if
we mean, in a looser sense, that something important is going on

because numerous men together are now engaged in redefining for themselves and for their societies what it means to be a man, then the description may be accurate. A body of literature assessing masculinity—books, journals, newsletters—is emerging. Men's conferences, workshops, retreats, and organizations are appearing on the scene. Men's studies programs have emerged at hundreds of colleges and universities. While the churches have not been in the vanguard of this movement, they are beginning to take notice. They are beginning to realize that deeply spiritual, theological, and ethical issues are at stake.

This unmasking of the male experience can be a confusing array of quite disparate things. It can be an exciting and hopeful journey. It can be a painful and angry process. It can be tender and deeply personal. It can be privately self-focused or highly political. It can be socially transformative or reactionary. In any event, it is almost certain to be confusing. What, after all, are the real problems? And how do we go about changing things? The present ideological divisions of the men's movement in the United States betray the confusion. Though the spectrum is broad and the ideological points along the way overlap, three broad positions have been emerging.

The most conservative and often reactionary group in the American men's movement sees feminist women and the abandonment of traditional gender roles as the central problem. The "free men" and "men's rights" groups are tired of the guilt they feel feminists are laying on them. They do not want to be blamed for everything that goes wrong in the world. Further, many of them have specific complaints about their own oppression. They feel threatened by job competition from women in the marketplace. They feel discriminated against by "affirmative action" hiring policies. Separated and divorced men often feel abused by the courts in matters of property, child custody, and alimony. While professing to want change, the men's-rights males want to turn the clock back. Traditional gender roles were better. And though speaking about a new masculinity, sometimes this group strangely betrays an antimale bias: the male is still in need of taming by the more spiritual and domestic woman.

A second ideology presently is receiving considerably more public attention. It comes from the "mythopoetic" group, so-named because of their reliance on the images of masculinity found in ancient myths, poetry, and fairy tales. They might also be called "the masculinists," because they see the core problem as the loss of an archetypal masculinity that men once possessed. This loss has resulted from the alienation between fathers and sons, the absence of other male elders to mentor young men, and the disappearance of male initiation rituals. The solution is the rediscovery of "the deep masculine" through male bonding and initiation rituals suggested by ancient myths. The central figure and inspiration of this group currently is poet Robert Bly, whose interpretation of the mythic fairy tale "Iron John" has captured many male imaginations.

Though professing that they are not antiwoman, many masculinists resent much they see in feminism. The women's movement, they believe, is convincing too many men that the feminine archetype equals life and nurture while the masculine archetype equals violence and domination. The results are alienating men from their own true natures and creating a pervasive hostility to men. Further, too many younger men are being lured into an emasculated spirituality that produces the "soft male"—peaceful, perhaps, but devoid of energy and sexual vitality, awash in a lingering confusion of perpetual boyhood and committed to a female mode of feeling. Thus, Bly and others urge men to recapture the deep, life-giving masculinity of the Wild Man. Through grief work over their losses and through male-bonding initiation rituals, they try to uncover the masculine archetype that lies deep within.

I find much of importance in what the masculinists are saying. They show admirable sensitivity to men's need for male-male intimacy. They clearly name men's hunger to reconnect with their fathers. They recognize young men's need for elder male mentors. They rightly name men's need to grieve for many real losses. They understand the power of community and ritual life. They know the importance of masculine energies.

Yet, I worry. The mythopoetic masculinists often show little grasp of patriarchy's continuing distortions of our lives. They seem not to recognize how much our masculinity has been constructed on antiwoman and antigay perceptions. While insisting that their central images of the Wild Man and the warrior do not mean a brutal war-making or earth-destroying man, the masculinists do not vigorously address the alarming amount of male violence in our world.

The component of the American men's movement that I believe most constructive and authentically hopeful might be called the "men's liberationists." This group also takes seriously the personal hungers and needs of individual men. It too is concerned with the litany of "what men want." Several emphases, however, distinguish this group.

Men's liberationists take seriously the feminist critiques of patriarchy. They recognize that personal change in men also requires political change. They see that while grief work is important, it must not turn into a whining victim ideology. They understand that we must move beyond warrior images and stop the violence. They know that gentleness is not softness and that masculine strength is displayed by lovers of the earth. Their ideology consciously rests on a threefold affirmation: it is pro-male, but also pro-gay and pro-woman.

This third orientation in the men's movement is the most accurate in understanding the problems and most genuinely hopeful in the directions for change, both personal and social. The reflections that follow in these pages, I hope, will illustrate that.

The root of the problem, I believe, is that we have not yet dealt very well with some deep problems in the social construction of masculinity. British sociologist Victor Seidler correctly concludes that "masculinity is an essentially negative identity learnt through defining itself against emotionality and connectedness."[1] It is important to add something to this, however. *Current masculinity is too largely a negative identity because it is grounded in male body alienation.* We men have defined ourselves over against emotionality and connectedness *precisely by* defining ourselves over against femaleness and homosexuality— for to heterosexual men it is women and gay men who most clearly symbolize the body. This approach, strangely, applies to gay men as well as to nongays, for in heterosexist societies all of us, regardless of our orientations, have been taught an antifemale, antigay meaning of masculinity. That this has had oppressive and destructive consequences for women and gay men has been demonstrated in previous chapters. What I want to explore here are the destructive effects of this negative construct on *men's* own self-identity.

While this is not a new thesis, we who profess our grounding in an incarnational faith have not sufficiently explored it. And if it is true, then religious claims about the goodness of bodily life and about incarnation—the revelation of God in and through the body—will be of particular importance to men's healing and transformation.

Men and Aging: A Case Study

One way of exploring this thesis is to focus on a specific challenge in men's lives. While negative masculinity constructions and body alienation take their toll on men in virtually every arena of life, a particularly vivid example is seen in the experience of aging.

So let us turn to male aging as a "case study." Our task is twofold. First, it is to trace the negative sexual meanings and myths our society attaches to aging and to see the crises they engender in males. Second, it is to name some challenges concerning the transformation of male aging.

Listen to the aging poet:

> Too old for love and still to love!—
> Yeats's predicament and mine—all men's:
> the aging Adam who must strut and shove
> and caper his obscene pretense . . .
>
> And yet, within the dry thorn grove,
> singer to singer in the dusk, there cries
> (Listen! Ah, listen, the wood dove!)
> something conclusion never satisfies;
>
> and still when day ends and the wind goes down
> and not a tree stirs, not a leaf,
> some passion in the sea beats on
> and on . . .
>   (Oh, listen, the sea reef!)
>
> Too old for love and still to long . . .
> for what? For one more flattering proof
> the flesh lives and the beast is strong?—
> once more upon the pulse that hammering hoof?

> Or is there something the persistent dove,
> the ceaseless surges and the old man's lust
> all know and cannot say? Is love
>
> what nothing concludes, nothing must,
> pure certainty?
>
>   And does the passionate man
> most nearly know it when no passion can?
> Is this the old man's triumph, to pursue
> impossibility—and take it too?[2]

Thus writes Archibald MacLeish.

There is the predicament. Our youth-oriented culture finds little to celebrate in the aging process, a process we see as an unwelcome reminder of our fragility and loss. Hence, we marginalize older adults in a host of ways, of which sexuality is a major example. Reserved for the young, sexuality in the elderly seems (in the poet's words) either an "obscene pretense" or an "impossibility."

While this unwelcome rain falls on the just and the unjust alike, it usually lands more heavily on women in a sexist society. In an earlier patriarchy, Abraham and Sarah both laughed when told that they would have a son. They were laughing, however, not because of Abraham's age, but because of Sarah's. He was one hundred, she only ninety. The Hebrew scriptures did not consider it unusual for a man to father a child at such an age; it was a woman's childbearing at ninety that was preposterous. This ancient account in the Bible may be the first record of male-female sex differences in aging—and one of the first accounts of the sexual activity of older persons viewed as a laughing matter.[3]

In a widely quoted article some two decades ago, Susan Sontag reminded us that aging as a moral disease afflicts women much more than men. While aging can enhance a man with dignity and power, it renders a woman undesirable and ineligible. She must disguise her wrinkles, and a cultural standard of female beauty becomes her enslavement.[4] Today, aging still is at least as much a social judgment as a biological eventuality. True, there are biological changes, but what we do in constructing their social meanings is of greater importance.

In some other ways, however, our collective denial of aging

and our marginalization of the elderly affect both men and women alike. The cartoons, the birthday cards, and the jokes we all know display society's penchant for trivializing aging sexuality as both laughable and forgettable. Though I laughed heartily at a recent birthday card, it illustrates the shadow side of all of this: (On the cover) "You are aging like fine wine. With each passing day you grow more mellow, more mature, more full-bodied!" (Then inside) "Soon your cork will dry up and fall off. HAPPY BIRTHDAY!"

Medical professionals routinely neglect the elderly's sexual concerns, as do the churches whose denominational literature typically omits any references to their sexual needs and interests. In their embarrassment over the sexual and intimacy needs of their widowed parents and grandparents, adult children find subtle and not-so-subtle ways to discourage those interests. A self-fulfilling prophecy results. Older adults lack social permission to express their attraction to other persons, they fear appearing ridiculous or immature were they to reveal their sexual needs, they feel overwhelmed with confusing guilt feelings about their desires, and they finally cope with all of this by denying their own sexuality.

The results go beyond such personal confusion and damaged self-image. Correct diagnoses of medical and psychological problems become difficult. Family relations are strained. The administration of justice to older persons accused of sex offenses becomes distorted. All in all, our sexual marginalization of the elderly creates significant problems in social injustice.[5]

Sex and the Aging Male: Biological and Social Factors

What do we know about genital sexual capacity and desire in aging males? A number of facts are now well established:[6]

- Most older people, both male and female, are sexually active. While age brings physiological factors affecting the frequency and sometimes the form of activity, there is no reason to assume the inevitability of genital incapacity in the aging. Those who maintain regular sexual activity throughout their middle years are likely to continue in later years. Those who use it usually do not lose it.

- Men over fifty generally experience a decline in genital function, but for most it has been a gradual decline beginning in their early twenties. The frequency of intercourse, the intensity of physical sensations, the speed of attaining an erection, the erection's hardness and size, the force of ejaculation, and the sperm count all very gradually diminish. There is also a longer refractory period—the interval needed between ejaculations. But the desire and capacity to enjoy sex often remain unchanged.
- Male fertility continues into a man's eighties and nineties. While sperm production slows down, it typically endures into very old age. Though testosterone production gradually declines after age fifty-five or sixty, usually there is no major drop in male sex hormone levels. Only about 5 percent of men over sixty experience the male "climacteric," a condition of physiological and emotional changes resulting from low testosterone production.
- Aging men with female partners past menopause frequently find enhanced freedom and responsiveness in their partners simply because pregnancy is no longer a worry.
- Specific medical problems may inhibit male sexual functioning, to be sure. Such problems may include diabetes, severe heart disease, complications from hypertension medications, and arthritic mobility impairments. However, it is the psychological factors more than the physiological ones that typically inhibit sexual activity in older men.

Thus, biological factors typically are not the crucial problems. "The geriatric sexuality breakdown syndrome" is more typically the result of the internalization of certain cultural understandings about sex and the elderly. The aging male is particularly vulnerable to a paradoxical combination of those messages. On the one hand, his sexual self-image remains wedded to "youthful manly performance," and he often anxiously misinterprets his gradual bodily changes as meaning that sex is over, when in fact that is far from true. On the other hand, he is bombarded with cultural messages that his sex life ought to be over, and that he is a dirty old man simply for having sexual feelings. Hence, he may well repress those feelings out of the desire for social acceptance. The strange combination of messages is confusing, indeed.

In fact, the desire for sexual expression actually increases in many older people. Sex brings with it an enhanced sense of self-assurance and well-being, especially when other forms of personal gratification have decreased because of retirement, illness, or the death of loved ones.

Yet "the procreative norm" for justifying sexual activity still persists. Even though three hundred years ago Protestants began to turn away from reproduction as the justification for intercourse, and even though the large majority of Roman Catholics in our society practice contraception, the procreative norm is still applied to aging people. When baby-making is no longer possible, then lovemaking seems inappropriate for them. Gay men and lesbians who have long suffered negative judgments on their sexuality from this standard continue to be discounted in their aging.

Associated with this factor is the "Noah's ark syndrome" common to many churches. People are supposed to enter two-by-two, and congregations are couple- and family-oriented. Many aging persons, however, and the majority of the very elderly, are single.

Older heterosexual men are still more likely to be married than are comparably aged women. This phenomenon stems from several factors: the earlier average death age in men, the persisting tendency of men to marry women younger than themselves, and men's greater dependence on women for nurture and care than vice versa. Among elderly heterosexual males, those who are married tend to be happier and longer-lived than their single counterparts.

Older people frequently hide their sexual intimacy from the world. They hide because they have long internalized negative messages about their sexuality. They conceal their activities also because their children, who have never been able to envision their parents as fully sexual, likely will not approve of such in the aging parent. Remarriage may not be practicable for economic or other reasons. So, for reasons of both social disapproval and their own guilt, older persons end up hiding their relationships.

All these things now seem rather clear about sexuality in aging persons and, given our focus, particularly in men. But, does the

aging gay man experience them in the same ways as his heterosexual counterpart?

The Aging Gay Man

In some ways there are no differences in sexuality and aging
between gay and nongay men. The physiological issues are the
same. Moreover, one's general quality of life is often determined
less by sexual orientation than by the factors that affect all older
persons, such as the state of one's health, one's finances, and
one's social support. Yet there are some differences.[7]

In some ways, the aging gay man actually may have advantages over the nongay—advantages, paradoxically, that he has
been forced to develop because of his social oppression. He may
experience fewer emotional crises. Many married men first experience the crisis of independence in old age when their wives die.
However, the older gay man often has coped with aloneness
earlier and has developed the skills required for independent
living.

In addition, the aging gay man often has stronger friendship
resources for facing crisis. He has networks of male friends that
the heterosexual man often lacks. Even gay men who have had
long-term committed partners are less likely to retreat into
couple privacy and less likely to depend on the partner to satisfy virtually all their emotional needs than are the married
heterosexuals.

Another advantage is that the gay man is often less concerned
about maintaining a strong masculine self-image. Hence, he will
likely experience less stress about his masculinity when bodily
changes affect that self-perception.

Even so, the older gay man has all the predictable problems of
living in a heterosexist society, problems that are often heightened in the later years. Frequently, the hospital or the nursing
home does not treat his partner as a spouse. Legal and insurance
systems discriminate against him in wills, property inheritance,
and insurance benefits. And, though his masculinity may seem
less threatened by bodily changes, his aging body sometimes
makes him subject to discrimination by those particular gay male
subcultures that place strong emphasis on youthful attractive-

ness. Finally, to the usual stresses of aging are added the big and little oppressions that the gay man has experienced every day of his life in a homophobic and heterosexist society.

Living by the Laws of the Afternoon

These, then, are some of the biological and social factors that often affect the sexual experience of the older man. Let us now turn to certain broader meanings that accompany his aging, meanings that are still sexual and bodily.

We have had enough sugary and unrealistic talk about "growing old gracefully." As David J. Maitland reminds us, a more honest depiction of aging sees it as a series of important and difficult tasks to be resolved, and sometimes those tasks are spiritual crises. But aging is not just a cruel joke perpetrated by our Creator. It is an opportunity, if approached in a countercultural fashion, that challenges the conventional wisdom about these things.[8] Thus, we are once again invited to reconstruct and reshape some of the major meanings that we men have associated with male body life.

Carl Jung once noted that different things matter at different stages of our lives, and those things which mattered early in life are not necessarily as important or appropriate in later years.[9] What was true in the morning becomes a lie in the afternoon. We follow the laws of the morning in the afternoon of our lives at the peril of our souls. The laws of the morning, according to Jung, place an emphasis on the external rather than the internal. They insist on control. They prefer parts of the self rather than the whole. And they place an unrelieved confidence in the human will. The laws of the afternoon, in contrast, have an internal focus. The work we are about in this chapter—exploring the sexual meanings of the male aging process—is a crucial part of honoring those laws.

Though he was attempting to make general observations about human experience, Jung, I believe, described men's experience more than women's. The external emphasis, the high value placed on control, the focus on parts of the self—these in our culture are more characteristic of men at certain stages in their lives. And they give shape to certain problems with which the aging male must cope. Three interconnected problems typically loom as crises, all related to body image: performance, loneliness, and mortality. Each of these three seems to interweave with the other two.

When Freud was asked what a sane, emotionally healthy adult would look like, he replied that such a person would be able to work and to love. While there is much truth in that observation, our traditional gender roles greatly complicate the picture. Why? Men have been defined by work, and women by love. If that seems an oversimplification regarding today's younger adults, it is still largely descriptive of older folk, whose gender meanings were primarily shaped in an earlier day. Even for younger men, the grip of older meanings is still strong. Men of working age who have no employment outside the home are judged far more harshly than women whose work is located only in the home. Women who are more dedicated to their careers than to their families are judged far more harshly than their similarly oriented male counterparts. Men can stumble at home but must not fail at work. Women can fail at work but must not do so at home. Men work. Women love. And both sexes are diminished.

Work makes a man! And it is not simply work as such, but performance. It is success at work. Though men are diminished by such a masculinity test, the good provider and breadwinner images are still critical for male self-esteem and identity. Men's fear of failure at work is often an extremely powerful motivation. If I fail at work, others will discover that I am a fraud as a man.

The problems of finding masculine identity through work performance are legion. Some forms of work are unsatisfying, monotonous, dehumanizing, or dangerous, and men's anger at such jobs that are supposed to give them dignity and meaning is often translated into violence at home.

Further, the identity a man receives from his work is often competitive and isolating. Titles of recent best-selling books directed toward business success leave little doubt of this: *Swimming with the Sharks; Winning Through Intimidation; Looking Out for Number One.* Loneliness becomes a companion to performance success.

Now, in his aging, a man begins to let go of his occupation. Retirement comes, sometimes eagerly embraced, sometimes reluctantly accepted. In either case profound adjustment in his self-image is usually required. Work no longer claims the hours or the urgency it once did. He is no longer productive by the reigning standards of his society. Now identity is no longer so tied to the job. But what is he as a man?

Work performance and sexual performance anxieties frequently come together in the body meanings of the older man. For years, youthful images of sexual performance, virility, and phallic prowess were an important part of his cultural measures of his manhood. But now the genital signature of masculinity ("two feet long, made of steel, and it lasts all night") is less true of him. And work performance is largely ended. The hard-hitting executive who played hardball at work all those years may no longer be hard at work. And sexually he is no longer quite as hard. Performance masculinity as measured by sex and work is under threat.

In addition, it is the time of life when loved ones are lost through death or separation. Loneliness becomes more a possibility, and it too is full of sexual meanings—for he experiences it as a man. Both my mother and my mother-in-law have lived in a large retirement home near us. I have eaten in the dining room there numerous times. In that retirement facility a small minority of the residents are men, most of them widowed. They usually cluster together at the same tables when they eat. I have observed them frequently and find it sobering. Though five or six are sitting together at the same table, they seldom carry on any conversations during the meals. Indeed, they seldom speak to one another at all. After all, what is there to talk about?

Mortality anxieties, performance fears, and loneliness all interweave. A couple of years ago I discovered to my relief that my sixtieth birthday had come and gone very peacefully—a relief, because I had had a terrible time the decade earlier turning fifty. The day before my fiftieth, the young checkout clerk in the neighborhood co-op food store glanced at me and asked, "Are you eligible for a senior discount?" That didn't help. Neither did it help a day later on my birthday, halfway through my jogging course, to be grasped by the terrifying thought that I might have a coronary before I got home. No physical symptoms were present, but the ominous fear was very real. In a moment I was able to laugh at myself, but I did walk the rest of the way home. Fifty felt ominous. My father had died suddenly in his fifties. A very close male friend had died a few months earlier, three days short of his fiftieth birthday. Now it strangely seemed like my turn, and the menace felt real. Astute psychologists have long known the deep inner connections between sexuality and death, and literature is full of the interplay of Eros and Thanatos. Anthropologists tell us that societies often cope with mortality anxiety through sexual regulations. It is not surprising when men are in control. A man's genital experience reminds him of his finitude. In intercourse, he experiences erection and then, after ejaculation, loss of erection—life and death. A woman seemingly goes on and on.

Further, remember a common difference between men and women—so common that it scarcely attracts our attention. It is the experience of profound bodily changes. Bodily changes can frighten a man because they are so foreign to his experience. He has never menstruated regularly, nor has he been pregnant, given birth, or lactated—all profound bodily changes. Death is the most striking change of all, and he is not prepared. Moreover, death is the final challenge to bodily invulnerability, to linear thought, to self-control, to mastery, and to winning. It is the final impotence, the utter defeat of hardness and performance.

For all of us, but particularly for men—and particularly for aging men—to recover our earthy finitude is, paradoxically, a way of both embracing our mortality and loosening its anxious grip. Though we have not experienced the cycles of menstruation, we males can embrace our own cyclical nature. Birthing and dying are part of the divine plan. In recovering the pleasures of finite body life, we might also learn that touch and sensuous pleasure are a major antidote for violence. There is now convincing evidence that body-positive societies are predictably more peaceful than are body-negative ones.

Performance, loneliness, and mortality—three intertwining realities with which the aging man must deal. When he is sexually disfranchised by cultural mythology, his dealing with those realities is made infinitely more difficult. But when he can know that his sexuality is blessed in particular ways in this time of his life, his engagement with those crises can be creative. He may come to know grace more profoundly, for he can accept himself for who he is, quite apart from the need to justify himself by his work or his works. He may come to know that loneliness is a signal that the Divine Lover has created us for intimacy, not self-sufficiency.

In celebrating the pleasures of finite body life, perhaps the older man may increasingly experience a kind of "existential love," a love that is intensely here and now. If in some earlier years sexual pleasure was linked more to hearth and home and visions of the future, now it seems more to bring the tender and poignant awareness that life is transient, that our days are numbered, that pleasure is particularly keen in the moment, and that life is more precious precisely because it is fleeting.[10]

At one point in Christopher Fry's play *The Lady's Not for Burning* there is concern that a child, Alizon, might be missing. Margaret worries that she might be lost. Nicholas's response is this: "Who isn't? The best thing we can do is to make wherever we're lost in look as much like home as we can."[11] That might be a clue. Perhaps there is more capacity to be at home in this crazy, anxious, beautiful, violent, tender world precisely because we know that this life is fleeting and not final in its meaning.

A Counterculture Church for the Aging

The trivializing of the aging person's sexuality by our society has very little factual biological basis, and it is a cruel hoax to perpetrate, particularly when aging persons may well find in sensuous intimacy a profound renewal of their self-worth. When in an ageist culture we challenge those social constructions of sexuality and masculinity that divest both men and women of creative power to live fully in their aging, we are doing important countercultural work.

While the church is often complicit in cultural judgments, there are hopeful signs of its awakening to a transformative, countercultural vocation with and on behalf of the aging. Though aging is always a very personal experience, we dare not forget that the personal is political. Thus, the final word must be a reminder of how social all these issues are. Consider these items for the church's agenda:

1. We can challenge and change our churches' uncritical sanctification of the nuclear family.[12] We have been complicit in equating a relative and fairly recent historical development with God's eternal will. That family idolatry still manifests itself in the ways we organize our congregations, in our language of worship, in our Christian education materials, and in our family-night suppers. And that idolatry can only reinforce the older person's sense of loneliness and deviance from the norm.

2. We can transform our antisexual spirituality into one that is body-affirming, eros-positive, and sensuous—a spirituality that expresses the good news of the incarnate God. The churches' continuing sex-negativity exacts a heavy cost from the aging. Despite official denominational statements, our reigning pieties all too frequently still endorse a procreative norm that grants "exceptions" from general sexual prohibitions only to married heterosexuals of childbearing ages. Then we continue to stigmatize and sexually disfranchise the elderly, for whom touch and physical intimacy may well be more important than ever before in their lives.

3. We can reexamine our theologies and practices of marriage in ways that can bless cohabitation by committed couples for whom legal marriage is financially prohibitive.

4. We can make congregations a safe and honored place for same-sex relationships. This is crucial not only for lifelong gay men and lesbians, but also for many formerly married persons who are drawn to same-sex relationships in later life.

5. We can affirm the gift of sexual self-pleasuring in the elderly single, many of whom have been reared with consistently negative messages about masturbation and bodily self-love.

6. We can encourage health care personnel who are church members to affirm and support the sexual and intimacy needs of the aging in their medical and institutional settings. We can assist our institutions for the aging to make adequate provision for privacy space where residents can freely express emotionally and physically intimate relationships without fear of discovery and shame.

7. We can nurture men's support groups in our churches, groups in which aging men will find new avenues for friendship and self-expression.

8. Finally and significantly, the churches must challenge the economic system that sustains so much destructive mythology about the aging.[13] The nuclear family is surviving, though with some difficulty. It is surviving in part as a consumption unit, but usually on the basis of two incomes. Working adults find it very difficult to sustain older family members' full participation in the family intimacy system. This, in turn, contributes to the crisis of loneliness.

Furthermore, our capitalist production and consumption economy still strongly governs our basic values about human worth. The economy says that individual fulfillment (particularly for males) must be measured by standards of performance and work success. When persons pass beyond a certain point of productivity they are assumed to be marginal, and our economic system reinforces their sense of powerlessness. Losing a sense of their power, they need more and not fewer loving and sensual relationships as they age, but they often perceive themselves as less capable of those relationships.

In all these ways, and doubtless others, our churches might yet heed the call to become vigorous advocates with and for the aging. It is a call to transformation within church life itself. It is also the call for churches to embrace their vocation as social pioneers in society. When that happens, more of us will be able to claim the words Dag Hammarskjöld wrote in *Markings:*

> " — Night is drawing nigh —"
> For all that has been — Thanks!
> To all that shall be — Yes![14]

6

Revelation in Men's Experience: "I Need—I Hurt—I Can't"

Perhaps three of the hardest things for many men to say are:
"I need . . ."
"I hurt . . ."—and
"I can't."
How often those words have stuck in my throat when I wanted to say them! Surprisingly, those phrases may be clues to our fuller experience of—indeed, embodiment of—God's presence. I suggest that we test those three difficult phrases against a trinitarian insight into God's ways of being God: as our Creator, our Redeemer, and our Sustainer. There may be paradoxical revelation in men's experience. In our own difficulties, the divine just might draw near—with a surprising reinterpretation of our experience.

"I Need"—The Creator

First, "I need." This expression is a clue to the Creator, who yearns for embodiment in our lives. Recall how the African American poet James Weldon Johnson pictured the creator God as needy:

> And God stepped out on space
> And he looked around and said:
> I'm lonely—
> I'll make me a world.[1]

Out of loneliness, out of vulnerability, comes the Divine Lover's creation. Out of need, not divine self-sufficiency. To be sure, that is not how we men have usually imaged God. We have imaged God as utterly self-sufficient, needing nothing. Hence creation was sheer gift. It is gift, indeed, but most traditional interpretations have left creation with nothing to give back to the Creator, for God was without need.

The image of God without need has emerged from phallocentric theology. And what are the values of *phallos,* the prized erection of male virility? "Big, hard, and up." We project those genital-sexual values onto our experienced worlds. Indeed, as we have seen, in "a man's world" the adjectives "small, soft, and down" simply pale by comparison.

We then project these values onto God. God created us in the divine image, and men returned the compliment, creating "him" in our masculine image. Now God's sovereignty becomes a big-hard-up kind of transcendence. Because we embraced a masculine model of self-sufficiency, we also conferred the same on God. Thus we envisioned God's perfection as divine completeness, needing nothing.

The legacy of a one-sided phallic masculinism has given us God far too frequently imaged as unilateral, nonrelational power, a power glorified by human weakness and dependency. Then, because we have attributed to God a one-sided power, we have compensated for that with a one-sided and unilateral understanding of the divine loving. If God is absolute power, we have reasoned, then God must also be sheer agape, love that is only self-giving and never needing to receive. For how can such power exist without destroying us fallible, sinful people unless it is mated with utterly forgiving agape? In the process of this kind of theologizing, we largely lost the possibility that God's love (and ours) might also be erotic.

No wonder we who are men—having modeled deity after masculinity and then masculinity after deity—find it difficult to say, "I need . . . I am vulnerable." Yet as bodyselves we are constantly needy and vulnerable. We hunger. We hunger for breath. We hunger for food and thirst for water. We hunger for touch and closeness, and we yearn with the desires of love. We become ill. We become disabled. We age. We are needy and vulnerable beings. That awareness is God's revelation to us through our body life.

Yet, growing up as a boy, I was taught differently. Early on I was taught that certain body feelings were not acceptable. Stiff upper lip, old man. Big boys don't cry. Be a good soldier. Good soldiers put on their armor, and so did I. I learned to defend myself against all bodily attack and any attack on my feelings. As did many boys, I learned my lessons well.

When we lose touch with our body feelings, we lose touch with God's own vulnerability, and when we lose sight of God's vulnerability, we lose the blessing for our own. Nevertheless, the Bible is full of images of divine desire. The Hebrew scriptures know God's yearning for connection with the life God has created. Thus, Hosea pictures God as the parent reaching out in hunger for connection with her child:

> When Israel was a child, I loved him,
>   and out of Egypt I called my son.
> The more I called them,
>   the more they went from me.
>
> . . . .
>
> Yet it was I who taught Ephraim to walk,
>   I took them up in my arms;
>   but they did not know that I healed them.
>
> . . . .
>
> How can I give you up, Ephraim?
> How can I hand you over, O Israel?
>   (Hos. 11:1–3, 8)

The Christian scriptures are marked by the passion story—literally a story of God's creative, hungering, life-giving passion. Other religions (particularly Buddhism, Hinduism, and indigenous Chinese religions) speak of God's playfully ordering the universe, of God's intimate love of beauty, and of God's fertile warmth and desire for union.[2] We have yet to imagine the implications of the divine Eros.

Resistance to our own neediness has made masculine theology

suspicious of both eros and self-love. Recently I was invited by two different churches to preach sermons on sexuality. Both sermons were given to large, well-educated city congregations. I used texts from the Song of Solomon, texts celebrating God's gift of our sexuality. I suspect that few in those churches thought the sermon theme inappropriate, even though it was seldom heard from the pulpit. I suspect that most were open to the suggestion that divine grace might be powerfully experienced in lovemaking with one's beloved. But when I suggested that masturbation might also be a means of grace, I think I heard gasps. In each congregation I received several comments that the "M-word" was a shock, and that some folk had expected lightning to strike the pulpit. Now, to be sure, we no longer view this subject with the horror of nine-teenth-century physicians and sexual purity reformers. Yet, sexual self-pleasuring is still an arena of guilt even for the "enlightened," simply because it somehow seems too self-centered, too imma-ture—indeed, too self-loving and too needy.

Such body attitudes, however, may be a clue to our spiritual-ity. When we, especially we who are men, divorce ourselves from our embodiedness, when we try to live as manly spirits simply inhabiting body-machines, we live by an illusion. Then we are disconnected from the changes, the needs, the vulnerabilities of the body. We have only the illusion of control. We have no need for self-love. And then, strangely, the possibility of deep connec-tions and emotional intimacy with others becomes problematic.

I understand vulnerability as the capacity, sensitively and imaginatively, to enter into another's story and appropriately to welcome the other into one's own. It is a capacity that draws richly on the affective, on the imagination, on the poetic, on the intuitive. It is a capacity profoundly linked with body connection and with the bodily revelation that we are needy. God said, "I'm lonely—I'll make me a world." When that capacity in us is alive and well, the presence of the creative, creator God is in us and in the relationship.

"I Hurt"—The Redeemer

The second phrase so difficult for many men is "I hurt." I suggest, however, that here too is a paradoxical clue to God—the Redeemer.

In spite of some signs that men today are better able to express feelings than were their male elders, there is still much discomfort when a man openly shows pain, grief, fear, or just plain hurt. When on rare occasions we let those feelings out, we typically follow with an apology: "Sorry, I didn't mean to cry. I don't know what came over me."

We need not look far for additional illustrations. We who are men are in the distinct minority of psychotherapy clients in our society, though there is no indication that our levels of mental health are better than women's. Indeed, there are numerous emotional stresses to which we are much more subject. Still another sign: When a newspaper prints a picture of a crying man, it can expect angry responses from readers denouncing such insensitive invasion of privacy—a reaction virtually never forthcoming regarding a photo of a crying woman. Alan Alda has a hypothesis. The problem, he believes, is "testosterone poisoning."[3] Somehow, we males have just gotten too much of the stuff. Testosterone poisoning is cruel because its sufferers usually do not know that they have it. In fact, when they are most afflicted, then they think they are most attractive and at their healthiest. In fact, they give each other medals for having advanced symptoms of the illness. While Alda makes his suggestion with tongue in cheek, his description of the results has some accuracy.

The reality is that most men today still live in a cultural atmosphere with little tolerance or support for their pain or grief. We have been taught from childhood that some feelings (like aggression) are acceptable for men, but other feelings (like helplessness) are not.

This supposition is not a good recipe for healthy grieving. If we have learned to be self-sufficient, dependency makes us anxious. Then it is hard to ask for or receive support. So, currently, about 80 percent of the participants in grief groups facilitated by hospitals, hospices, and private therapists are women. We have equated our masculinity with keeping on the move and solving problems, while the experience of grief would make us turn inward and slow down—an unmanly thing to do. As psychotherapist Alan Wolfelt observes, "It is very much in vogue today to encourage men to openly mourn. However, simply urging men to mourn does not adequately address [such factors]."[4]

I have referred earlier to my own problems in dealing with mortality. For years the best I could do was to treat death abstractly or with humor. I was reasonably adept, for example, at talking about the varied Christian perceptions of death and resurrection, noting their contrast to Greek understandings of immortality. Or, with Woody Allen, I could joke, "I don't mind the thought of dying—I just don't want to be there when it happens!" But until I faced the long-unresolved grief work surrounding my father's sudden death, I could not let the mortality issues become truly personal. And in holding them off I allowed them to hold me in their grip.

Most men have much grief work yet to do and find it difficult to do it. For many men this grief work involves reconnecting with their fathers, whether the father is still alive or long dead. In Samuel Osherson's phrase, we are still carrying "the wounded father" inside us—an image of the father who was punitive, or weak, or incompetent, or sick, or tyrannical, or—quite likely— just plain absent, not there for us. And that wounded father affects our sense of masculinity.[5]

Searching for positive clues to male identity, a boy discovers that his father (if, indeed, his is a two-parent family) is more physically and emotionally distant than his mother. Moreover, his father's messages about manhood are counsels of separation: Be your own man; keep your guard up. The mother's world felt like the soft, moist, timeless world of the body, the world of holding and caring. The father's world feels different. It conveys prestige, power, and control. At the same time it also feels like distance, performance demands, and separation. The boy's boundaries now separate him from intimate connection with others, but also distance him from his body and feelings.

The blessing from my father that I had sought but not received was the clear message that I was loved for who I was, not for any performance or achievement. My unresolved anger was linked to my father's absence, but also to needless emotional and physical abuse received at his hands. My unrequited yearning was to reconnect, to have the prodigal son and the prodigal father finally embrace and tell each other, "I love you"—words never before spoken. After many years of resistance to grief work and then after several years of therapy, some of that reconnection has occurred. I now know something of being blessed by the redeemer God in ways that I had not known for many years. And some reunion with my long-dead father has taken place.

I also now realize that during those many years in which I resisted my hurt, anger, and grief, I was disconnected from my body in myriad ways and thus severed from a whole range of feelings. I literally did not cry tears for twenty-four years.

All our relationships are mediated through our bodies. It is in our emotions that we interact with the world. Our senses and bodily integrity ground our relatedness. When the body is deeply alienated, dis-eased, we lose our sense of connectedness to one another, to the world, and to God.

Many Christian understandings of the cross and of divine atonement have compounded our confusions. Current feminist theology reminds us that when a righteous father God is depicted as requiring the suffering of the Son to appease the divine righteousness, such understandings easily become images of divine child abuse.[6] Such images distort the relations of human fathers and sons.

Far truer is the realization that only a God who says, "I hurt," can help us. Then it is God who is hurting, not God requiring the Son to hurt to satisfy somehow the Father's honor. Then both parent and child are aching for each other. That is quite different from one impregnable in perfection and the other powerless to earn the parental favor, yet striving vainly to model the parent's "holiness."

Somehow, only when I know that God hurts can I admit my own pain. Only then can I live deeply into all parts of my own story and into the stories of others. All of this has something deeply to do with that mysterious affirmation of faith: "I believe in the resurrection of the body." Our bodyselves are now alive to joy precisely because we have become open to our pain. Because we have become open to our pain, we find our pain shared and carried in the very Heart of the universe, who has robbed death of its cruel victory.

"I Can't"—The Sustainer

A third phrase that is difficult for me and, I suspect, for many other men is "I can't." This phrase might be another paradoxical revelation of God—now God as our Sustainer. The sustaining God is always the empowering God.

However, "I can't" is a man's admission of powerlessness. The words are difficult to say, for our conditioning is to be "can do" men. In the process of that conditioning we learned a certain understanding of power. It was power as potency—phallic power, the capacity to inflict our will on others.

What alternative revelation might come through the male body? For illustration, I focus on the genitals, inquiring of their revelatory meanings.[7] I know that men simply genitalize far too much sexual feeling. Nevertheless, part of the problem is not genitalization as such, but rather its one-sidedness. The form of male genitalization has been overwhelmingly phallic, and hence partial. When part of reality is absolutized there is always distortion and idolatry. Fearing impotence and death, we have undervalued our penile softness as revelation, though flaccidity is our condition most of the time. We have undervalued our testicles as bearing revelation—"balls" as both symbols of manly courage and our most vulnerable body part. The undervaluing of our genital softness and vulnerability, and the overvaluing of the phallus take their toll on everyone, men included. One cost to men is our loss of a significant kind of spiritual energy and power. It is the energy and power associated with the Via Negativa. It is different from the Via Positiva, the dominant form of Western spirituality over the centuries. The Positiva is the way of light, the way of transcendence, the way of climbing to God. The Negativa is the way of darkness, of emptying, of sinking into the sacred depths. This way, strangely, ushers in a fresh kind of sustaining power. Dietrich Bonhoeffer discovered the power of the Via Negativa while in prison awaiting execution by the Nazis. God, he wrote, is teaching us that we must live as those who can get along very well without God. The God who is with us, paradoxically, is the God who forsakes us. This is the One we no longer need as our rescuer, the "deus ex machina" who waits in the wings ready to swoop onto the stage of our lives and get us out of trouble. But God no longer needs our religious practices and pieties begging for divine aid. "I should like to speak of God," wrote Bonhoeffer, "not on the borders of life but at its center, not in weakness but in strength, not, therefore, in [our] suffering and death but in [our] life and prosperity. . . . The Church stands not where human powers give out, on the borders, but in the center of the village."[8]

While this affirmation may seem contradictory to the revelation of the God whose own hurting redeems our pain, it is not. Bonhoeffer is not denying our need, our vulnerability, and our pain. He is not denying the divine suffering. Rather, he is decrying those theologies that see God primarily as the occasional rescuer, as the answer to the questions in "the boundary situations" of our lives, and as the One who enjoys our human powerlessness. God is to be celebrated at the very center of our lives, not on the edges.

Moreover Bonhoeffer is making the paradoxical assertion that it is precisely in divine powerlessness and suffering that a new kind of power is revealed.

> God is teaching us that we must live as men who can get along very well without [God]. . . . God allows [Godself] to be edged out of the world and on to the cross. God is weak and powerless in the world, and that is exactly the way, the only way, in which [God] can be with us and help us. . . . Man's religiosity makes him look in his distress to the power of God in the world. . . . The Bible, however, directs him to the powerlessness and suffering of God; only a suffering God can help.[9]

We who are men are here invited into empowerment through a fresh revelation of what power actually is. For a variety of reasons, we have come to believe that the phallus is the emblem of masculinity, the signature of true maleness. This is only partly true, and partial truths taken as the whole truth become demonic and destructive. Thus we have come to believe that power is one-way power, top-down power, the capacity to influence others while being minimally influenced ourselves. We have come to believe that size or stature in this kind of power is a quantitative thing characterized by coercive strength and maximum self-sufficiency. We have been taught that power is limited in its quantity. It is a "zero-sum" game—the more you get, the less I have.

This kind of power is shaped more by individual boundaries than by relationships. Ronald Reagan, the cowboy actor and American emblem of manly power, became president. As president he effectively both symbolized and appealed to such understandings of individualism and male power. Part of that effectiveness lay in his triumph over his own body. He looked youthful in spite of his years. He could joke just after being shot, could turn his failing hearing into an asset, and could chop wood and ride horses when his contemporaries were taking to their rocking chairs. We learned that a powerful man was in control of things, and body control significantly symbolizes control over much else—feelings, relationships, work, life.

However, such power severely curtails our understanding. Understanding requires vulnerability and reciprocity. It requires sinking and emptying. When I control my body, I develop little understanding of my emotional life, and then when my emotions really take hold, I am likely to be overcome by them. When I perceive myself as in control of others, I am unlikely to enter into their subjectivity. The controller knows little of the subordinate's feelings and perceptions of the world, while the oppressed have wide eyes. That is why liberation theologians speak of "the epistemological privilege of the oppressed"—one simply knows more when one sees from the underside.

There is another kind of power. It is relational and generative. It does not aim to control or to diminish the power of another. It aims at mutual empowerment. It is willing to be influenced as well as to influence. Its ideal of size is not quantitative, but qualitative—the size of the soul. As Bernard Loomer has taught us, it is your soul when you can take a large volume of life into your being while still maintaining your integrity and individuality. It is the intensity and variety of outlook you can entertain in the unity of your being without feeling defensive or insecure. It is your power to encourage others to become freer in the development of their own diversity and uniqueness.[10]

The good news is that there is generative power in sinking, emptying, letting go, in saying "I can't." In those moments we meet the empowerment of the sustaining God. Again, we cannot escape the paradox. The sustaining One is not the omnipotent Deliverer, waiting in the wings to rescue us from trouble. More truly, this is the One who is "in the center of the village," in the center of our lives *as bodyselves.*

In another letter from his prison cell, Bonhoeffer wrote:

> God requires that we should love [God] eternally with our whole hearts, yet not so as to compromise or diminish our earthly affections, but as a kind of *cantus firmus* to which the other melodies of life provide the counterpoint. Earthly affection is one of those contrapuntal themes, a theme which enjoys an autonomy of its own. Even the Bible can find room for the Song of Songs, and one could hardly have a more passionate and sensual love than is there portrayed.[11]

Revelation and Miracle

Three difficult phrases: "I need . . . I hurt . . . I can't." Strangely, they can be "good news for modern man."[12] Strangely, those words open us more fully to the embodied presence of the One who is our Creator, Redeemer, and Sustainer. When this happens, we are more reconnected as the bodyselves we are. And Christ is present, often in the unlikely and in the unexpected. When that happens, there is a miracle of grace in the midst of the everyday that helps us to celebrate the Word still being made flesh and dwelling among us.

I witnessed such a miracle. A few months before Bill died, he and Bob phoned us one Sunday afternoon. On that particular day, my wife's eighty-two-year-old mother was visiting us. Coming from a lifetime in small-town South Dakota, she had never knowingly even met a gay man. Bob and Bill were phoning to say that they would like to drop in with some bran muffins and brownies they had just baked.

We told Mother they were coming. She had known from our previous mention of these friends that they were gay. Before they arrived, we told her, in addition, that they both had AIDS and that Bill did not have much longer to live. We felt it important to tell her that, for Bill would clearly show the ravages of his illness—the racking cough from pneumocystis, the lesions of Kaposi's sarcoma, the wasted body. She deserved the opportunity to be prepared.

They came. We were not sure what Mother's reaction would be. Wise and caring in so many ways, yet her long years had not prepared her for this encounter. She was, after all, an elderly woman from rural South Dakota, never aware of having met a gay man, and now she was meeting two, and both with AIDS. How would she react? We did not know.

When they entered the living room, Mother did not remain seated, though her age would have justified it. She got out of her chair and went to greet them, extending her hand. The five of us visited for an hour or so. Bill and Bob then departed, leaving their gift of bran muffins and brownies. Soon after they left, we three sat down for a light Sunday evening supper. Their gifts of food were on the table along with a few other things from the refrigerator. With all the common fears about AIDS transmission in the public mind, we did not know what Mother would eat. The conversation centered around their visit. She wanted to know more about these two men, and finally said, "I'm really glad I was here to meet your friends." Then, rather deliberately, "I believe I'll have one of those bran muffins." She ate two, and finished with a brownie, as did each of us.

Never before or since has the Sacrament been more real to me: the broken bread coming from Christ's broken bodies—and giving life. And never before in my experience had the Holy Sacrament included brownies.

Both Bill and Bob are now dead, but they were bearers of grace. They still are.

7

Men as Pastors and Counselors: Manly Pitfalls and Possibilities

Some of you reading this book are religious professionals who counsel others as part of your work. I address you specifically in this chapter. Others of you, however, whose work does not regularly place you in the counselor role, might still find some personal connections in what is to follow, for we all carry stories within us that we tell to others.

Anton Boisen, a pioneer in the field of pastoral care, spoke frequently about "the study of living human documents." He meant that the stories of persons' struggles with their emotional and spiritual lives demand the same respect from pastors and religious counselors as do the stories and historic documents of our faith. Each living human document has an integrity of his or her own that calls for compassionate and insightful interpretation.

That same insight applies as well to those of us who are pastoral caregivers, as Charles Gerkin reminds us. More than anything else, we are listeners to and interpreters of stories. Thus, we do not come empty-handed to the other person's story. We too are living human documents, the bearers of stories.[1]

Two of the stories through which we present ourselves to
clients, counselees, parishioners, patients are our gender stories
and our faith stories. Consider the intertwining of these two,
particularly in the male experience.

Gender Stories

First, there is the gender story. Some of us were born male.
Immediately upon our emergence from our mother's womb
someone—a doctor, nurse, or midwife—looked between our
legs and said, "It's a boy." That was our sex. From that moment
on, people began to teach us, both consciously and unconsciously, what it meant to be a boy and destined for manhood.
Out of those teachings and learnings we constructed our gender.
Born male: our sex is biological. Taught to be masculine: our
gender is socially constructed. Now, as adults, those who are
males bring both manly problems and manly possibilities to
pastoral care. And what is "manly"? Webster defines it simply as
possessing the qualities that are generally regarded as those that
a man should have. Then Webster adds examples such as virility,
strength, bravery, honor, and resoluteness. The dictionary definition, likely written by men, both paints a positive picture and
gives a heavy assignment.

As we reflect on the interplay of sex, gender, and pastoral
theology, one obvious problem, named earlier in these chapters,
is this: we who are men have been slow in coming to self-
consciousness about the issues of our masculinity, for we have
been blind to much of our own experience as men. Let us
continue our process of unmasking that experience, asking now
about our male body stories as shaped by our gender learnings.
Recall Baby Suggs's counsel: we've got to love our flesh, love
it hard (see chapter 3). Do men really need this advice? Do we
not love our flesh? After all, part of manliness is a good body, so
we jog and pump iron—good manly stuff. And yet we treat
our flesh all too instrumentally. A book title provides an illustration: Shortly after the amazingly popular women's book *Our
Bodies, Ourselves* was published, a men's book with similar
format came out. Its title was revealing: *Man's Body: An
Owner's Manual.*[2] There it is: the body is like a car—something
to own, use, and keep in good operating condition for maximum

performance. For a variety of reasons, we men have learned some profound ambivalence about our own embodiedness. As a corollary, we live with surprisingly mixed feelings about our sexuality.

We are proud of our sexuality; after all, sex is what makes a man a man. Virility and courage are of one piece: "He's got balls." But we are also anxious about our sexuality. The thought of impotence can paralyze us, and the perception of women or gays as more sexual than him both frightens and angers the heterosexual male.

We are easily confused about intimacy. Because we have genitalized so much of our sexual feelings, intimacy and sex seem to be one and the same. Thus, if we are heterosexual, we fear intimacy with other men because it seems to imply genital expression. And deep emotional intimacy with women threatens our masculinity, because we learned our first lessons about manhood by the process of breaking the erotic bonding with a woman, our mother.

We have been taught to love sex and body pleasure. We have been taught that a real man can never get enough of it. A man is always ready for sex, and never has a headache. Yet the ways we learned sex in our youth were not the ways of nourishing and pleasuring our whole bodyselves, but rather were physical releases of sexual tensions. We learned to measure those releases with performance statistics in competition with other males.

These are some of the rather common sexual-body experiences of men in our culture, experiences that give considerable shape both to images of masculinity and to male theology. What we are about in Part Two of this book is the task of unmasking our male experience, because we who are men have become invisible to ourselves. To do useful body theology we must move deeply into our body experiences and put them into dialogue with our experiences of God's reality.

Faith Stories

That brings us to a second story that is carried into pastoral caregiving. It is the faith story. Christians claim an incarnational tradition. With the writer of the Fourth Gospel, we say, "In the beginning was the Word, and the Word was with God, and the

Word was God" (John 1:1). When the Word came to dwell with us, it became—what? A book? A creed? A theological system? A code of morality? No—to the everlasting embarrassment of all dualistic piety, it became flesh, and it continues to become flesh. Thus, our commitment to an incarnational faith presses important questions on us.

- Are there ways of affirming the centrality, the paradigmatic importance, of Jesus as Christ without denying that christic potential, the possibility of embodying divine presence in human flesh, to everyone else?
- Are there ways to release the Christ from the tomb of doctrine that would limit the christic reality to the singular divinity of Jesus? Are there ways we too can express and experience the real meeting of divine and human?
- Are there ways of freshly affirming an Easter faith, that Christ is, indeed, alive? that Christ is alive not only in "spiritual form" but also in flesh?
- Are there ways that we who are men might participate in the resurrection of the body—our bodies?
- Are there ways men might freshly experience and communicate the christic reality, the communion of divine and human loving, in the midst of pastoral caregiving?

Differing religious traditions symbolize incarnation differently. We who are Christian name the Christ. Unfortunately, our Christologies often point more to disconnection than to connection. Under the impact of a dualistic Greek metaphysics, the church's Christology became too largely an abstract doctrine about the singular divinity of Jesus. He was understood to be the unique and only genuine occasion of the joining of the divine and the human. The result was to confine christic reality to that one person and to deny it to everyone else. However, Jesus' intent was not to control or monopolize the Christ presence. It was precisely the opposite: to share that reality with all who would respond.

In what came to be the orthodox view of Jesus as Christ, what was so often lost was the understanding that incarnation is the invitation to everyone. What was substituted was the belief in an unchanging God of perfection, whose divine love was utterly different from human love, whose divine body was utterly different from human bodies. Lost was the compelling experience of divine incarnation as the meaning and reality and life-giving power of every authentic relationship.

What if we recover the christic reality as a possibility for all of us? Then we might have to take with some seriousness Luther's statement about being "Christ to the neighbor." And, at least as frequently and more important, we might recognize the neighbor being Christ to us.

There will be times when we sense that somehow we are the embodiment of healing, power, and connection for another. When it happens we can only give thanks, for in our better moments we know that we are not the source of that connecting power. The source is God. But we have been in that moment the necessary meeting place of God and human flesh, the crucial, even if fragmentary, embodiment of God.

At least as frequently, there will be times when the other—counselee, parishioner, or patient—is Christ to us. It is "the Matthew 25 phenomenon"—"Lord, when was it that we saw you hungry, thirsty, a stranger, naked, sick, in prison?" Here is the stunning reversal. Christ is in the wrong place! We are not the Christlike therapists armed with strength, techniques, and professional skills to cure. Now it is the Crucified One who is in the ditch, in the hospital bed, in the counselee's chair. Now it is the one who reminds us of God's absence who paradoxically mediates God's presence. Now it is he or she who mediates God's vulnerability and weakness, thereby eliciting our own. In our mutual need we are, for the moment, bonded in life-giving communion.

It is still the christic experience. It is still the embodied God. It is still the meeting with the cosmic love in and through human flesh.

It is precisely this experience which reminds us that genuine ministry to persons is the art of making space for others to grow. As James E. Dittes writes, "[It] requires becoming a vacuum that enables others to loom large. Ministry is the constant sharpening and shaping of questions more than the giving of answers . . . in going, radically, to the people as they are, rather than insisting that the people come to the minister."[3] This space-making,

self-disclosing ministry of vulnerability may well be more difficult for men than for women. But it is an invitation to us all. And
it is a ministry requiring us to do theology because of the body,
the body of Christ—the body that is not exhausted in our
individual bodies as we meet each other, but that surrounds us
with a great cloud of witnesses, the universal church.

Gerkin puts it well: "Pastoral care is . . . that relationship to
the other person which seeks to open both pastor and parishioner to glimpses, signals, signs of God's presence, to engender
the quality of expectancy of God's disclosure."[4] In other words,
by modeling our expectation of God's disclosure in the intersec-
tion of our human stories, we participate in the divine story.
And, I would add, if the divine story is one of incarnation, we are
participating in the risen Christ, the continuing embodiment of
God.

Moral Contexts of Pastoral Counseling

Bearing in mind the interweaving faith and gender stories that
are part of both pastor and parishioner, counselor and counselee, now let us turn to the pastoral counseling process itself.
Consider first some of its moral dimensions, inescapable moral
contexts surrounding the interaction of its story-bearing participants. I would like to name four.

First, *the fundamental purpose of counseling is a moral one.*
That purpose, simply put, is to help make right something that
has gone wrong. The parishioner, or client, comes with a problem (might we even say the person is *de-moralized?*) and the
therapist assists the person with different ways of understanding
his or her life situation. The aim is both a fresh way of defining
what is desirable and empowerment to realize something new.
As contextualists like to insist, the real stuff of ethics is not
principles or rules, ideas or abstractions, but relationships.
Counseling is one important mode of dealing with wounded,
broken, or underdeveloped relationships with others, with the
self, and with God. So the basic reason for counseling and the
"stuff" of which it is composed constitutes a moral context.

Let us call the second context *the theological-ethical commitments in the counseling method itself.* Whether done by a religious or a secular practitioner, counseling is necessarily based on

interpretations of the purpose of life, the causes of human difficulties, and the dynamics of human change. Counseling is always a religious or quasi-religious enterprise, with theological and ethical assumptions about creation, the purpose of life, human nature, sin, and redemption embedded therein. Indeed, as many have argued, the very definition of mental health itself is a profoundly religious and moral enterprise.

For example, one assumption that inevitably enters the counseling relationship is the place of self-love or self-regard. The influences of Carl Rogers, Abraham Maslow, and Erich Fromm have led many of us to emphasize the importance of self-regard in regaining personal power and health. But as Paul Tillich years ago and Don Browning and numerous feminists more recently have pointed out, this important debate about the place of self-regard in human life has not been just a narrow psychological debate. It has been a basic discussion of the ethical foundations of human relations and of the nature of human loving.[5]

A third moral context involves the counselor's basic attitudes and actions regarding *respect and coercion*. If the general aim of counseling is to assist the parishioner or client in changing something—perceptions, feelings, actions—the issues of respect and coercion are always present. How much of counseling is persuasion, obvious or subtle? When does the therapist know best? When is informed consent essential, and when is it truly informed and consenting?

Sexuality issues enter significantly here. When and how is physical touch appropriate? The recent, much-needed discussion of "the unmentionable sin"—sexual abuse of women clients by male counselors—is the obvious case in point. But sexual abuse can be subtle as well as blatant. When a counselor reinforces stereotypical gender-defined roles or allows homophobic biases and anxieties to intrude into the counseling relationship there are moral issues of coercion and abuse.

The fourth general context is the *moral community*. Again, Browning has persuasively argued that pastoral care has as a central task the incorporation of members into the meanings, goals, and distinctive life-styles of the church.[6] To focus pastoral care or counseling simply on handling individual crises or interpersonal strains is to neglect the moral community itself and is to capitulate to an individualistic, secular therapeutic ideology. The church, after all, is a bearer of a moral worldview. It is a place for moral discourse and decision making. Pastoral counseling is thus founded on a whole context of moral meanings, values, and norms expressing the religious community's best lights regarding how life ought faithfully to be lived—in our economics and politics, in our families, in our sexuality, in our interpersonal relations, in our environmental responsibilities, and all the rest. Pastoral counseling takes seriously the integration of the individual into the life-style of a faith community.

Here, then, are four moral contexts of pastoral counseling. They are not "levels" in any hierarchical sense. Rather, they can be visualized as overlapping contextual circles, each implying the other and all having significance for counseling as a moral process.

The Body in Pastoral Counseling

Now, consider one particular moral issue. It is theological as well, as all moral issues are. It is an issue frequently neglected in counseling. Its significance is sometimes missed even by pastoral counselors committed to an incarnationalist faith. The issue is *the body.*

Most of us have known times when we felt at one with our bodies. Then we felt vibrant and alive, sensually at one with our surroundings. We had little sense of separation between the selves that we are and the bodies that we are. There was little feeling of living in a temporary home, little sense of bodily deadness, shame, or pain. Unlike Saint Francis, who preferred to call his body "Brother Ass," we felt one in body and soul, harmonious and integrated. We were secure and at home in the world.

However, those times have been too few, too fleeting, too fragmentary. In fact, we often do not realize how "dead" parts of our bodies are. We become accustomed to our tensions, our pains, our lack of bodily sensation. They have become so much part of us that they seem natural.

Thus, our ambiguous histories live in and through our bodies. Part of that history is unique to our own particular past relationships and experiences. Sometimes we body forth our histories in dramatic ways. The "type A" coronary patient and the person struggling with anorexia or bulimia are only more noticeable examples of what is true about us all.

Not only our unique personal histories live in us bodily, but also our shared religious and cultural histories. In earlier chapters we have seen how the remarkable sense of bodyself unity in Hebraic experience was, in spite of Christian incarnational faith, distorted by the spirit-body dualism that entered the church's thought and practice from the late classical world. The subsequent periods of our religious body history are fascinating and mixed, but they are variations on the same themes: the struggle between the unitary view of the self and a view of the self split between the higher and lower parts; the struggle between the faith that joyfully embraces creation and the faith that longs to escape the flesh to another world; the struggle between the incarnational conviction of God's continuing embodiment and the conviction that God is "wholly other," eternally distant from creaturely life. Such religious ambiguity is part of our history, and it inevitably lives in our bodyselves. Such ambiguity is part of both the faith stories and body stories we bring into the counseling relationship.

What has been happening in psychological understandings of the person as embodied? Edward W. L. Smith opens his book *The Body in Psychotherapy* with these words: "The mind-body dichotomy has been so entrenched in Western thought that to consider the 'mind' to be the bailiwick of the psycho-therapist and the 'body' the bailiwick of the physician seems perfectly logical to most Western people."[7] I fear that there is considerable truth there. Counselors frequently focus on what is happening in the head and leave the body to the physician.

To be sure, the modern psychotherapeutic tradition does display some elements of a more holistic perspective. In certain ways, the founding giants recognized it. Freud observed in 1923 that the ego is "first and foremost a body-ego . . . ultimately derived from bodily sensations."[8] Alfred Adler was long interested in the body's capacity to compensate for both physiological and psychological damage. And while Carl Jung wrote little about the body in therapy, his patients frequently danced, sang, acted, modeled with clay, and played musical instruments during treatment. Nevertheless, most modern depth psychology contin-

ued to understand personality disorders as rooted in a disembodied *mind*.

There were exceptions. Before his work lost credibility with
many, Wilhelm Reich developed a significant way of seeing
character as a total body phenomenon. Reich's influence bore
fruit in the Gestalt therapy of Fritz and Laura Perls, Franz
Alexander's body therapy, Alexander Lowen's bioenergetics,
and the dance therapy pioneered by Mary Starks Whitehouse, to
mention a few. Indeed, a "body therapy technology" soon arose,
spawning its own denominations and sects, its orthodoxies and
heresies. The human potential movement picked up a good bit of
this, and some of us personally profited considerably from the
experience. But the focus was heavily on practical technique, and
body insights were not deeply probed for their religious and
social significance. Even the more holistic therapists of fulfillment, such as Carl Rogers and Sidney Jourard, though well
aware of the inseparable connections of body and mind, did not
press a truly incarnational approach.

A more direct assault on our dualistic understandings of
health came from the feminists. In the first edition of *Our
Bodies, Ourselves*, fourteen members of the Boston Women's
Health Book Collective said this of their exploration:

> The experience of learning just how little control we had over our
> lives and bodies, the coming together out of isolation to learn
> from each other in order to define what we needed, and the
> experience of supporting one another in demanding the changes
> that grew out of our developing critique—all were crucial and
> formative political experiences for us. . . . *For us, body education
> is core education. Our bodies are the physical bases from which
> we move out into the world; ignorance, uncertainty—even, at
> worst, shame—about our physical selves create in us an aliena-
> tion from ourselves that keeps us from being the whole people
> that we could be.*[9]

We have reminded ourselves of some of our religious and
psychological histories about the body. Now, what can we
understand of the body as a moral reality in pastoral counseling?
Surely, there are dimensions of body life of which the counselor
is usually aware. We know we communicate much with clients
through our own body language, and through theirs they tell us

a great deal about themselves and about how the therapeutic process is going. We are aware of the sexual feelings which at times both we and clients experience, and how these can affect the counseling relationship. Such body consciousness is important, indeed, but there is more to be said. Among a number of possibilities, let me suggest three interrelated moral capacities significantly rooted in body experience, capacities of enormous importance to both counselor and counselee: *moral understanding, caring,* and *connecting.* I am a white, middle-aged male, and my own particular experience will be reflected in my illustrations of these.[10]

First, *moral understanding.* I work in the field of theological ethics. Increasingly I am painfully aware of how much of Christian ethics is abstract, geared to linear logic, and hyperrationalized. Increasingly I am aware of the underdevelopment of imagination and feeling in my (male-dominated) field and, yes, in myself as a practitioner.

Here the recovery of bodily life is promising—no less to counseling than to ethics. The effective counselor draws deeply on the affective, on the imagination, on intuition, on poetic insight. The pastoral counselor no less than the ethics teacher wants to help people nurture their moral imaginations and make good decisions about their own lives and about the common good. Though we have not yet well integrated it into our Christian moral theology, psychologically we have long recognized that the affective is deeply connected to the body. Our abilities to know what we are feeling and really to feel those feelings are rooted in body experience. We recognize it when those capacities are damaged or underdeveloped. Thus, the sexually abused woman may deaden her body to a large range of feelings in defense against past and future pain. And we know that, generally, men just do not feel very well. I know what I am thinking more clearly than what I am feeling. What we must yet grasp is that disconnection from our body feelings is also disconnection from *moral* understanding, and that affective reconnection nourishes *moral* perception.

Our alienation—particularly male alienation—from bodily feelings takes a terrible toll. It leads us into abstracting ourselves from the bodily concreteness and reality of others. My abstractions lure me into an exaggerated, often violent sense of reality. They entice me to lose the concreteness of the present.

After all, my body life helps to shape my response to an often confusing world. I was conditioned by biology, religion, and society to treat my body as lower, foreign, as that which must be disciplined and controlled, as that which was irrational and must be mastered, as that which bore the intimations of decay and mortality—and it gave me a certain "feel" about the world. The world "out there" then took on some of the same confusing and half-known qualities. It was full of mysterious things that smacked of badness. I needed to sort things out, to make sure that I had a clear grasp on reality. As a result, I developed a penchant for neat categories that made ambiguous experiences more controllable. Often I responded more to categories than to persons.

Illustrations of such lost concreteness in the pastoral counseling situation are not difficult to find. The woman with a problem pregnancy becomes an exercise in sorting out ethical principles, and then the flesh-and-blood woman fades from view. Or the counselee becomes a psychological diagnosis. Or the grieving person is perceived as a series of stages. Or the lesbian or the gay man fades into the image of a genital actor and into theories about sexual orientation.

However, our recovery of incarnational reality promises otherwise. It promises that we might again use abstractions in the service of concrete life, not the other way around—the Sabbath was made for persons, and not persons for the Sabbath. It promises that contextual concreteness in counseling and in ethics will return. It promises that we will see freshly the relation of bodily life and moral understanding.

If our capacities for moral understanding are bodily in many significant ways, so also are our *capacities for compassion,* a second incarnational reality. Webster defines compassion as a deep feeling of sympathy for the sufferings of another, accompanied by a strong urge to help. It is not a bad definition. For once the dictionary is close to the biblical truth of the matter. The New Testament frequently interchanges "compassion" with "mercy." Numerous stories tell of suffering persons appealing to Jesus for mercy. These are appeals for deep sympathy, yes. They are also cries for help and healing. The Greek word describing Jesus' response is a strong term meaning, literally, "to be moved in one's bowels." In other words, it is to have the other's situation grab you right in the gut and to be moved viscerally to do something about it. The notion of compassion still remains abstract until we become incarnationally concrete and put human faces on the subject.

Consider one example that links the claims of both concreteness and compassion. It is abortion, an issue for both pastoral counseling and ethics. Criticizing his own Catholic tradition, Daniel Maguire wrote about his visits to an abortion clinic. Noting that while those who write on liberation theology frequently go to Latin America to learn, he observed that those male theologians who write on abortion usually stay at their desks. He decided to do otherwise. He obtained permission from a local abortion clinic to make a number of visits to observe and learn. He sat in on problem pregnancy counseling sessions and was struck by how vacuous the slogans of the debate are in the face of these concrete, living, human dilemmas. He held in his hand the plastic bag with the product of an abortion, and later reflected, "It was impressive to realize that I was holding in the cup what many people think to be the legal and moral peer of a woman, if not, indeed, her superior. . . . I have held babies in my hands and now I held this embryo. I know the difference. . . . We are more sensitized to embryos than to the women who bear them . . . [and] until we open our affections to enlightenment here, we will none of us be wise."[11]

If moral understanding and compassion are significantly bodily, so also is a third element of counseling: our *capacities for connecting*. The dualism that body ethics challenges here is the assumption that separation is more real than the connection—whether the separation between spirit and body in the self, the split between the self and the other, or the gulf between the divine and the human. The sense that separation is more real than connection is a particular issue for men. And it is one of the fundamental issues that pastoral counselors face daily with counselees.

In his well-known book *I and Thou*, Martin Buber said it simply: "In the beginning is the relation."[12] Not one, not I, not you, not even God, but the relation. "In the beginning is the relation" is a deceptively simple, yet radical, statement for the ears of anyone in a dualistic culture, particularly to those of us reared on the individualism of a Lone Ranger mystique. I am increasingly persuaded that the anti-body tradition in the Christian West is the basic cause of our blindness to the fundamental relationality of all life.

If we know anything at all, it is in relation to our bodily space. As we have seen, children learn the meaning of prepositions—in, over, under, between, beyond, beside, within—through an instinctive sense of their own bodily location in relation to the rest of their world. Indeed, as children we learn (until we are taught otherwise) that the fundamental reality with which we deal in life is not disconnected objects or beings, but relationships.

As infants we must literally be loved into being human. We must be given the human gift of relational capacity by being tenderly held, sensuously nurtured by the parental body, talked into our own speech, communicated into our own possibilities of communion. Pastoral counselors all too frequently see the evidence that the deprivation of this life-giving nurture is devastating.

Scientists see it too. One dramatic illustration has been provided by neurophysiologist James W. Prescott. His extraordinary cross-cultural studies have established the close connection between the physical nurturance of children and their later capacities for relationships. Children who are consistently held and affectionately and respectfully touched are significantly more inclined to develop later relationships that are cooperative, peaceful, and mutually respectful. Contrarily, the frightening evidence is that anti-body, antitouch, antisensual, antinurturing attitudes are strongly correlated with high levels of adult violence of all types. These correlations hold true not only for individuals but also for entire societies.[13]

Socrates counseled, "Know thyself." Surely, counselors have taken him seriously as it applies to their clients or parishioners. The goal of greater self-understanding rightly looms large in every relationship of pastoral care. It is also, as perceptive pastors recognize, imperative for themselves. But I know myself only as I know the profound relationality of my existence. I know myself only as I know the relationships through which my life is lived, the relationships that bring health, those which bring disease, those which can be transformed. To know myself as profoundly relational is to know myself as body, for all our relationships are bodily mediated. When there is bodily repression, when the body is deeply alienated and dis-eased, we lose our sense of connectedness to each other, to nature, and to God.

Through our embodiedness we see and visualize the realities around us. Through our emotions we interact with the world. Through our senses we experience what it means to be selves in relation. Our bodily, sexual, sensuous selves ground our relatedness. Our bodily integrity is the foundation of both our vulnerability and our power with others.[14] If these things have been problems for male pastors and counselors, they are also exciting invitations.

PART THREE

SOME
MEDICAL
ISSUES
FOR
BODY
THEOLOGY

8

Medical Care
and the Meanings of Bodily Life

A friend of mine, in the same profession as I, told me of an experience of his. He sat down next to a stranger on an airplane one day, and soon the two of them began to chat. Immediately, the other asked him that predictable man-type question, "What do you do for a living?" My friend replied: "I teach Christian ethics in a seminary." To which the other responded: "Christian ethics? That must be pretty simple. 'Love your neighbor as yourself'—I suppose that's about all there is to it, isn't that right?" My friend thought a moment and replied, "Well, yes, I guess that's true. And what do you for a living?" The other, rather proudly, said, "I am an astronomer." To which my friend responded (in one of his finer moments), "You are an astronomer. That must be rather simple. 'Twinkle, twinkle, little star'—I suppose that's about all there is to it."

The message of this chapter is, indeed, "Love your neighbor as yourself." But it is not quite that simple, and one reason is that "ourselves" and the "neighbors" we are to love are *bodies*. I do not just *have* a body, I *am* a body. I am always interpreting myself as a body, creating my meanings as a body, and using images and language to give significance to my bodily functions and dysfunctions, states of health and disease. Knowing that and taking that seriously contributes greatly to good medical care. Too often we have been taught by culture, by religion, and by medicine that our bodies are something quite different from our real selves. We have learned that our real selves exist in our minds or our spirits, while our bodies are but intricate machines. When we act on that assumption (whether we are medical professionals or just anyone experiencing disease) we do not relieve suffering, but rather compound it. However, when in situations of medical care we love our neighbors and ourselves as fully bodyselves, we likely experience relief from suffering and, at times, even from pain. That is the thesis I wish to explore in this chapter.

The *New England Journal of Medicine* rarely publishes poetry, but a recent issue includes these lines from "Modified Radical," by Ann Davidson:

> In bed her husband massages, oils, cradles
> both her breasts,
> especially the left . . .
> They lie together . . . and weep.
> No. Not flat
> her heart screams at night.
> legs not shapely,
> body not thin,
> it's her breasts
> that are beautiful . . .
> No one should see her . . .
> in her flat ugly sadness
> and shame.
> Unspeakable
> for a surgeon's knife
> to sever her breast,
> for him to scrutinize tissue
> and discard it in the trash.[1]

What are the meanings of the body in medical care? The meanings to whom? And why?

Body-Machine or Bodyself?

From days of antiquity, we have believed that physicians are obligated to relieve human suffering. Yet, even in the best medical settings with expert physicians, patients still often suffer not only from their diseases but also from their treatments. Observing this, Eric Cassel, M.D., comments: "Despite this fact, little attention is explicitly given to the problem of suffering in medical education, research, or practice. . . . The relief of suffering, it would appear, is considered one of the primary ends of medicine by patients and lay persons, but not by the medical profession."[2]

Why might this be so? Perhaps it is because we tend to confuse suffering and pain. Pain is organic. It is a bodily sensation. Dictionaries commonly agree that pain is sensation of hurting or strong bodily discomfort transmitted through the nervous system and caused by disease, injury, or functional disorder. Medicine in the West, under the impact of the mind-body split, has been particularly oriented toward physical bodies and their pain.

Then, what is suffering? It may be occasioned by organic pain, or it may not be. Whatever its cause, suffering involves a person's perception of the threat of disintegration—loss of integration. It is the distress accompanying events that threaten one's intactness, one's togetherness.[3] In her poem, Ann Davidson was not expressing pain. Yet in anticipation of her mastectomy she was, indeed, suffering. The coming loss of her left breast—"flat ugly sadness and shame"—would threaten her own coherence as a self. It was unspeakable that this treasured breast would simply be analyzed and then discarded in the trash. Nevertheless, in sickness and disease it is not always a simple matter to treat others and ourselves holistically. We have been shaped by a long history of spirit-body dualism that conditions us to be good splitters. Christianity did not invent that dualism, and, on the basis of its own central teachings, the church should have known better than to embrace that philosophy of the ancient classical world. Yet in many ways the church joined the cultural disjunction and passed it along.

The spirit-body split found powerful articulation in the writings of René Descartes, who in the seventeenth century laid the philosophical foundations for modern medicine. Descartes applied a mathematical model to organic bodies. The human body, he said, is nothing more, nothing less, than a complex machine governed by its own laws. Like a machine, it is subject to analysis and to the repair of its malfunctioning parts. Descartes's dualism was liberating for science. It provided a neat division of labor and let the new modern science escape the control of the church. Now the nonbodily realm of spirit could be left to the church and the physical, bodily world could be science's own domain.

Organic matters now became the physician's focus. These were the most real, the most clinically significant, the most worthy of attention. The patient's *illness* was thus transformed into a *disease*, a recognizable entity in the medical classification system. The doctor's concerns now were the symptoms, the disease etiology and history, the pathophysiology, and the possible treatment interventions. The body-object perception still finds its words whenever we refer to "the hysterectomy in room 421" or "the appendectomy in 207." There are not persons in those rooms, but rather bodies with dysfunctional parts.

Hand in hand with all of this, we came to think of physicians as high priests of the body and clergy as high priests of the soul. While that sounds like a neat and efficient division of labor, it persists in splitting the human being into two realities and distorting the very nature of the healing process. How does this work out in practice?

Human sexuality is a case in point, doubtless because it so dramatically exemplifies the body-spirit unities we essentially are. Consider the many ways sexuality is typically neglected as a significant health care issue:

- Nurses have difficulty teaching female patients breast examination procedures.
- The coronary patient's anxieties about future sexual expression are perfunctorily answered by handing him or her a pamphlet.
- The woman visiting her male gynecologist feels detached from her body by the impersonal, cold, clinical procedures and language.

- The victim of a spinal-cord injury spends months in rehabilitation before anyone even broaches the subject of sexuality.
- The dying cancer patient, subject to distressing bodily disfigurement, craves touch and intimacy, but finds no one to talk to about these needs.
- Double beds for couples in hospitals or nursing homes are virtually unknown.
- Lesbians and gay men often cannot get good medical counsel on many things because their physicians are so uncomfortable with homosexuality.

Sexuality is only one major example (though a striking one) of ways in which the conventional wisdom of body-spirit dualism affects our medical understandings. This is not to say that the medical model *necessarily* treats persons simply as bodies in need of repair. It is to say that we have been *strongly conditioned* toward perceptual leanings in this direction.

One might argue that body-spirit dualism is not all bad. In life generally, we admire the person who can set aside the body's needs to respond to other things that are more urgent. For example, the athlete who disciplines the body into a finely tuned machine invites our admiration. In health care, had the body not been objectified, we might not have the sophisticated clinical and research medicine we now enjoy. By studying the body as a complex machine we have achieved an amazing understanding of its biological gears and nuts and bolts. Further, some kind of practical dualism seems useful for both doctor and patient. It facilitates the doctor's focus on the body's adversaries (the guilty organ or the infectious agent), and it helps the patient understand what has gone wrong with his or her body. But while this approach can address pain, it cannot deal with suffering. While it can address the causes of and interventions for disease, it cannot address the meanings of the illness to the person.[4]

The phenomenon is exaggerated in medical specializations. To be mastered, a surgical procedure must be repeated a thousand times. The specialist has little time for things beyond the scope of the specialization. Colleagues usually ask no questions beyond the narrow scope of the specialty, and would be upset if

broader advice were given. In the process the patient is sent to a
stream of interchangeable white coats, whose wearers are not
personally recognized.

However, I do not just have a body. I am my body. My whole
sense of self is rooted in my body. It is the way I express myself
with others in the world. My body is me-acting. To be treated as a
body-machine instead of a bodyself compounds my problem when
I am sick. Illness itself threatens my unity as bodyself. When I am
sick, I lose some of my capacity for acting in the world. A curious
thing happens. I become more aware of my body, and yet I become
distanced from it. If when I am ill I am asked, "Are you your
body?" I will deny it. I do not want to identify with my malfunctioning flesh, which, for the time being, is in the charge of others.
My body seems very much with me, yet remote. My pains and
dysfunctions make my body feel foreign and thinglike. In such a
time my words are truly significant: "I'm not myself today." When
I lose touch with myself by disidentifying with my body, my world
correspondingly becomes impoverished. When my body is not
intimately me, I find intimacy with others more difficult.[5]

The Sting of Death

This disidentification with the body has its roots in the pervasive fear of death on the part of both physician and patient, a fear
discussed in earlier chapters. In many ways, death appears to be
the enemy, indeed, according to the apostle Paul, "the last enemy
to be destroyed" (1 Cor. 15:26). This is no news to modern
medicine. Our medical establishment shares culture's conventional wisdom that death is the enemy, and medicine frequently
magnifies this perception to mean that death is to be fought and
avoided at almost any cost. The tendency toward death avoidance in physicians, especially male physicians, seems apparent.
The penchant for life extension during the dying process, in spite
of prolonged physical pain, emotional distress, and financial
cost, is still all too common.

The unconventional, countercultural wisdom that the church,
the body of Christ, might bear on all of this is a different insight
into the reality of death and dying. The clue, I believe, lies in
Paul's words (1 Cor.15:55–56):

> "Where, O death, is your victory?
> Where, O death, is your sting?"
> The sting of death is sin.

There is, to be sure, a sting of death simply in the ending of life, in the facing of the inevitable cycles of nature, in seeing and experiencing the decay of the bodyselves that we are. But the real sting, as Paul rightly saw, is sin—the sense of alienation, of separation, of loneliness, of disconnection, of estrangement, of feeling cut off.

Yet that is the sting of illness as well as of death. Our hurts, our pains, cut us off from one another and isolate us. Pain makes us retreat into a lonely and private world. When we are sick, our pain causes difficulties for those who care for us but who do not share our pain, a reason why chronic illness is such a burden. Pain causes us to sense a loss of power over our own destinies. We become dependent, and we resent that dependence. We become vulnerable to the power of others over us.[6]

Our modern medical system, in a variety of ways, plays into all of this and frequently augments it, heightening the sting of death in its very attempts to avoid death. And how? We define an appropriate "sick role" for persons who are ill, a role they ought to play. Because sickness of any sort is a reminder of death, and serious illness is a prelude to death, we insist that those who are sick act in certain ways if the rest of us are to tolerate them. And what must they do?

- They must, by their words and behaviors, admit that illness is bad and something to be overcome.
- They must be obedient to the prescriptions of the medical professionals who tend them, thus placing themselves in a dependent, subservient position.
- They must submit themselves to long periods of isolation from others, and not insist that their loved ones stay around the clock in the hospital with them.
- They must not band together (unionize?) with other sick people to try to control their lives more effectively.

The list could go on. The point is that conventional wisdom and practice frequently increase the sting of death by heightening sin—sin now understood as separation, isolation, dependency, and powerlessness—in illness.

Here, then, is the problem. The connection between self and body, so important for our sense of wholeness and well-being, is fragile and tenuous in our time of illness. At the same time, the identity of the self with the body is an important element in healing. When a patient gives his or her body over to the physician as an object to be cured (like handing your car over to the mechanic and saying, "Here, do what you need to do to get it working again"), the doctor knows that restoration to health will be very difficult, if not impossible. If the patient's own self-healing energies are to express themselves, the patient must not have given up some sort of meaningful identification with her or his own body.[7]

Physicians and Suffering

In light of all this, what might be some implications for physicians' own professional self-understandings? In medical history the traditional view of the doctor's authority is usually traced back to Aesculapian tradition, so-named for Aesculapius, the Greco-Roman god of medicine. In this tradition, the doctor's authority is derived from two things: medical knowledge and skills, on the one hand, and commitment to the noble goal of healing, on the other. While there is much to say for this model, it does mean that the authority for the physician's work comes essentially not from the patient or from a covenant between patient and doctor, but from the doctor himself or herself. Further, this implies that an asymmetry, an inequality of power between the professional and the patient, is normal and necessary. After all, the patient has the disease, and the physician has the knowledge and the skills to cure it, and these things are very unequal.

Consequently, several things happen. When the patient is viewed primarily as a diseased body, the organic facts about the disease become the crucial data. The patient's own understanding of his or her illness is assumed to be irrelevant. In fact, the patient's understandings may get in the way of successful treatment. After all, do not patients often believe and do irrational things? Like going on self-prescribed vitamin C regimens for cancer? Or failing to take their prescribed medications? Or believing that their illness is due to moral transgression or divine retribution? Scientific medicine is *im*patient with such patients.

Now patients are assumed to be under obligation to accept their physicians' understandings of disease and healing, understandings that are usually organic. When physicians attempt to incorporate social factors about patients into their diagnoses, they usually do so assuming that, in addition to being medical experts, they must also be amateur psychologists and must add these factors to their medical knowledge if they are to treat diseases successfully.[8]

Or, when a chaplain or minister joins the team on a particular case, the doctors may welcome that, "not necessarily because they hold that religion has a special contribution to make on its own but because they hold that the minister can in fact aid in the *medical* treatment of the patient."[9] The minister, it is assumed, may be more successful than others in calming the patient, in explaining what is at stake, and in gaining the patient's cooperation with the treatment. Yet the medical model of the disease is still assumed to be adequate and normative. The net result, however, is that the patient's own understanding of the illness (the *meaning* of the disease) is neglected—and a heavy burden of knowledge and authority is placed on the physician.

These patterns are often expressed and reinforced in the daily language of medical discourse.[10] The language we use inevitably alters reality by *re*-presenting it and making the reality a reflection of the speaker's or writer's perspective. Think of one possible scenario of how the medical report evolves in a hospital. In the middle of the night, Ms. Smith comes to the emergency room and tells her story to the physician there. The doctor asks certain questions and organizes the information of her narrative to conform to the standard medical report format, subsequently presenting her "case" at morning report. A different staff doctor, with report in hand, later sees Ms. Smith and adds to the report. In the days that follow, her "case" is presented repeatedly at rounds, of course with her absent. And each time the report is given, the living presence of Ms. Smith is a bit more abstracted.

Now, it is surely true that this kind of medical reporting has value. The purposeful, orderly report is done in a style designed to organize potentially massive amounts of information about a person into compact, useful medical information. But its very genre tends to depersonalize. Two medical authors describe it in these words:

> [Interns] invariably "present" in the traditional format they have been taught since their second year of undergraduate medical education: chief complaint, history of present illness, past medical history, social history, review of systems, tests ordered and their results, assessment of problem, treatment, and outcome. The delivery is also predictable: face and voice become expressionless, speech is usually either gently deliberate or rapidly businesslike. The patient is seldom named. The intern, meanwhile, uses passive verbs to avoid first person direct references to him or herself.[11]

Doubtless a great many physicians do see the living subject beyond the text of the medical language. But the pressure is strong in the direction of abstraction. While it admittedly serves some practical purposes, such language and style can abstract both the living physician and the living patient as persons. Medical personnel can begin to believe in the objectivity of the case record and in the objectivity of medicine itself. The report moves in the direction of anonymity and authority. Feelings of doubt can be absolved. Ms. Smith becomes less a person with a story, a person interpreting her own bodyself and her illness. She becomes more the possessor of a body-object with an organically classifiable disease and prognosis.

When this happens it is difficult to deal with her as a suffering human being, for suffering is not simply organic. It is that very personal distress we experience when there is threat to our intactness as persons. Suffering is our interpretation of what is happening. What, then, if my suffering is seen by another as merely subjective, not really real, hence not within medicine's domain? Or if it is identified exclusively with my bodily pain? What is very real to me as a patient is then trivialized, and I feel diminished, depersonalized, and my suffering is compounded.

It is impossible to treat sickness as something that happens solely to my body, without damage to *me*. In medical literature, pain and suffering are often equated, but they are not the same. It is commonly believed that the greater the pain, the more suffering is caused. But that is not necessarily the case. It all depends on the *meanings* associated with the pain, the *interpretations* given those physical sensations.

For example, in giving birth a woman might experience both pain and suffering—pain because of severe physiological discomfort, and suffering because of distress over an unwanted child or anxieties about the child's health. Often, however, a woman experiences pain with little if any suffering, because her organic distress does not mean threat to life but rather promise. Or a patient may report that when she thought her leg pain was from sciatica small doses of codeine controlled the pain, but when she learned that it was the spread of cancer she needed much larger doses of medication for relief.

Patients can often tolerate writhing pain when they know its source and know it is correctable and temporary. On the other hand, patients report considerable suffering from less pain when its source and meaning is mysterious to them. Suffering increases when the pain is not validated by other significant persons. Now the body in its most intense presence becomes, paradoxically, disembodied and alien to the patient.[12] When I am sick I have an ambiguous relation to my body. It is intimately me, and yet it is foreign. When my body is in pain I am acutely aware of it. It is infinitely close to me, yet strangely alien, "beseiging me and clutching me in a deadly familiarity from which I am incapable of extricating myself."[13]

Sickness brings out my capacity for dualism, for splitting myself. At one and the same time, I know my embodied self more than I know any other living being or object, and the most mysterious thing in the world to me is my bodyself.

In my sickness, if I am conscious and if I am not overcome with pain, I still have some capacity to make choices. I still have some ability to interpret what all this means. I will choose either resignation or meaning. I will choose either to resign myself to the belief that my body is a foreign object, or I will decide to find personal meaning in my illness, and hence a measure of integration. My body is thus the portrait of my limits and my problems. It is also the canvas on which I paint my choices and record my powers of integration.

Remember that the choices we make are not always on the

level of deliberative consciousness. They are often in the deep, unrecognized dimensions of the spirit. But they are choices. We make decisions about our incarnation, that is, about the ways that we body forth spirit in the world. Paradoxically, my body is both what makes me uniquely myself (the shape of my face, my fingerprints and gestures), and what makes it possible for me to open to other people, knowing through relationship our ultimate oneness.

Here again the church has something to offer. To live in the body of Christ is to gain strength to open ourselves more fully to our sickness and to each other. The wisdom of "the body of resurrection" (as Paul considers the church) is that we are eternally connected to God, and hence to everyone and everything else. The resurrection vision is not simply, or even primarily, a trust in an individual's survival after death. It is fundamentally a conviction of the profound unity and interconnectedness of all of creation—in our birthings, in our illnesses, in our dyings, and in God's assurance that meaning will not be destroyed.

Again, what might this mean for physicians? Recall that the Aesculapian tradition assumes that the doctor's authority comes from knowledge and skills used in healing. It assumes the necessity of an asymmetrical, unequal power relationship between physician and patient. Combined with the mind-body dualism of Descartes, this tradition strongly encourages the physician to treat a body more than a person. When that happens, the patient's own bodily self-understanding, the patient's own interpretation of his or her illness, seems secondary, if important at all. What seems essential is knowledge of the organic nature of the disease and skillful intervention. However, the patient's interpretation of the disease may be at least as important as medical interventions in dealing with suffering and the quality of life.

Informed Consent and the Patient's Authority

There are encouraging signs, however, that a different medical model is emerging. In the United States this seems particularly evident in primary care medicine. The newer approach assumes that the patient's own interpretation of illness is vitally important to the healing process. The concept of *informed consent* is a clue to all of this.[14]

Insistence on the consent of the patient is a fairly recent development in the history of medical ethics. Informed consent is linked to the rise of modern experimental medicine and its potential abuses, abuses dramatically evident in the crimes of Nazi medicine. Since the Nuremberg trials we have generally acknowledged that valid consent rests on the patient's having adequate information, freedom, and competency.

Those physicians who still largely hold to the Aesculapian tradition will tend to treat informed consent largely as a verbal transaction—saying the right words and dispensing certain information. Yet those who embrace this "body expert" medical tradition are skeptical of informed consent. They worry about the harm that too much information can do, its irrelevance when the patient cannot understand medical details, and the lack of trust in the doctor that insistence on informed consent seems to imply.

Nevertheless, a different understanding of consent is emerging. Now it is not primarily a matter of verbal communication and information, but rather a relationship of collaboration and mutuality between doctor and patient. This understanding does not rest on naive notions of functional equality in the relationship; the doctor's technical expertise is fully acknowledged. Rather, it assumes the mutual humanity of doctor and patient in dealing with illness as a deeply personalized bodyself issue.

Consent is now, in its deepest sense, essential to the doctor's own authority to practice. The authority to heal now comes ultimately from *the patient,* and that means also from the patient's understanding of herself or himself as a body-person and the patient's interpretation of his or her own illness. Just as a teacher is not a teacher without students, nor a pastor a pastor without parishioners, so also the physician is not a physician without the patient's gift. "Physicians who recognize that their authority to heal comes from their patients are enabled to exercise power for their patients' well-being without compounding their patients' distress."[15]

Hospitality and Healing

Both medicine and its patients have two legitimate needs, the technological need and the human need. There are also two ways of viewing illness parallel to those needs: the view of the body-object (which addresses the technological need) and the view of the body-subject or bodyself (which addresses the human need). These are two possible perspectives on the patient, two ways of understanding the same reality. One focuses on localizing and isolating the offending pain. The other attempts to grasp patients in their totality and to understanding the meanings of their sufferings and illnesses to them. The perspectives are not antithetical. Both are needed.[16]

We ought not to minimize the stress of medical professionals who must live in constant contact with others' pain. The most sensitive doctors and nurses know well the limitations of their curing abilities. The most sensitive among them need largeness of spirit if they are to cope regularly with the smallness of spirit in many seriously ill patients. The church as body of Christ needs to remind the medical profession that caring is its central mission.

It is through caring that the power of illness and death is broken. Curing, thankfully, sometimes may take place, but caring is central. The ministry of presence breaks alienation. It is presence that relieves the sting of death.

The church has some experience in knowing the central mission of the hospital: it is *hospitality*. The linguistic connection between hospital and hospitality is no accident. Indeed, by the fourth century it was common for congregations to have "houses of lodging for strangers." These were the first rudimentary hospitals in the West. Caring for the stranger's ailments was part of their task, but central was their ministry of presence and hospitality. If too often the modern hospital is a place of isolation—isolating the sick from the rest of us—we can try to recover the central meaning of the original hospital movement. "The hospital is, after all, first and foremost a house of hospitality along the way of our journey with finitude. It is our sign that we will not abandon those who have become ill simply because they currently are suffering the sign of that finitude."[17]

In the late twentieth century many diseases can be cured. Even when they cannot, suffering can be alleviated. The hospital and the practice of medicine are moral commitments that the sick will not be abandoned as persons. Hospitals and medicine represent the commitment that persons will not be body-machines.

They will always be bodyselves, whose own stories are part of the story of every professional who enters into a caring covenant with them.

We have made a distinction between pain and suffering. Now, finally, let us recall that there are two meanings to suffering. One is, as I have used it, suffering as the threat to a person's own integration as a bodyself. The other meaning is suggested by the old English use of the word "suffer," as in the King James version of Jesus' words about the children, "Suffer the little children to come unto me." The meaning? Let it happen. Go with the action. Take the experience into the center of your own being. To be fully present with persons as they move from suffering in the first sense to its second meaning is a profound invitation, challenge, and privilege of medicine and all those who care for others in illness.

Here are words from the story of another woman with breast cancer, whose suffering as disintegration became suffering as reintegration. Audre Lorde writes:

> At times, I miss my right breast, the actuality of it, its presence, with a great and poignant sense of loss. . . . Right after surgery I had a sense that I would never be able to bear missing that great well of sexual pleasure that I connected with my right breast. [But now] . . . I have come to realize that that well of feeling was within me. I alone own my feelings. I can never lose that feeling because I own it, because it comes out of myself. . . . I would never have chosen this path, but I am very glad to be who I am, here.[18]

9

Reproductive Choices: A Couple's Personal Reflection

With Wilys Claire Nelson

Note: This is our personal story. We write it in the third person to avoid the frequent and awkward repetition of our names. However, the cast of characters is simple: feminine pronouns refer to Wilys Claire, while masculine ones refer to Jim.

A Couple's Reproductive Story

They were a rather typical couple. Married in 1953, during the Eisenhower years of "normalcy," when women and men knew who they were and couples knew what marriage was about, they found little reason to question the going assumptions about reproductive choices. They took a number of things for granted, among them these:

- They would have children after about two years of getting to know each other. Prior to that, they would use birth control.
- Condoms or the diaphragm were their contraceptive alternatives. Their choice would be the diaphragm, since condoms made a man feel "like taking a shower with a raincoat on,"

and he didn't like that. Thus, birth control would be her
responsibility, and that seemed appropriate.

- They would probably have four children—preferably two of
  each.
- Once a conception was desired, it would probably happen
  soon. But if it did not and if the doctors could not help,
  adoption was the only possibility. They were only vaguely
  aware of artificial insemination and assumed it would not be
  chosen by responsible people. Newer forms of reproductive
  technologies had yet to be developed. But there were plenty of
  adoptable babies, if it came to that.
- After becoming pregnant, she would work for about six
  months and then stay home to prepare for the baby.
- They would not know the sex of their baby until its birth.
- During childbirth, she would be unconscious, and he would be
  outside in the fathers' waiting room. They knew no one who
  had had a cesarian delivery, so that possibility seemed neither
  a threat nor a promise.
- She would not work outside the home after the children
  arrived, at least until they were in school, and not then unless
  it was economically necessary.
- They would not consider abortion an option for an unplanned
  pregnancy.

Some of their expectations came to pass, though with more
difficulties than they had expected. Other assumptions proved
more complicated than they had imagined.

After a couple of years, they abandoned the diaphragm and
began trying to conceive. Contrary to their expectations, nothing
happened for a year. The physician began testing her for oviduct
blockage. When the doctor found nothing wrong, he gave the
couple advice about thermometers and calendars. He did not
suggest taking the husband's sperm count. Infertility, they all
assumed, was likely to be her problem.

After two years of the couple's trying, she conceived. Living in
an urban area where natural childbirth procedures were emerging, they learned of this option. She attended classes during her
pregnancy. He was with her in the labor room, and, contrary to
their earlier assumptions, she watched the baby being born. He

was not permitted in the delivery room, however, nor did they expect that. They were pleased by the amount of sharing in the process that they actually had, and they understood that delivery rooms were not meant for fathers or friends.

Two weeks after giving birth, she was taken to the hospital for an emergency appendectomy. He was left at home with a new-born infant. Since their parental families lived halfway across the country, responsibility for the child was all his, and yet he was totally unprepared for this kind of fathering. With the help of a few neighbors, advice from the doctor, and a copy of Dr. Spock for constant reference, he and his infant son survived the week of his wife's hospitalization, during which time he took his son to his wife each day to be nursed.

Some time later, she was given her first postbirthing pelvic exam by the male physician, of course in the presence of a female nurse. At the end of the exam, without any words about its contents, the doctor handed her a small brown paper bag containing a new diaphragm.

They were surprised to discover that in Connecticut in the mid-1950s it was illegal for anyone to prescribe or sell contraceptive materials. In order to secure the contraceptive gel for use with the diaphragm, she had to drive across the state line to the nearest Planned Parenthood clinic in New York State. Though she made this trip regularly during the next couple of years, she knew of no one else from New Haven who was doing this. One did not talk very openly about such things.

Their second child was conceived accidentally and earlier than they planned. After their daughter's birth, they decided (contrary to the prevailing expectations for good middle-class families) to have no more children. One of each was sufficient, and she went back to her diaphragm.

Two years later, now living in a different state, where contraception was legal, she began taking a new and experimental pill that her new doctor prescribed. Once on the pill, she experienced a great sense of freedom. There were no more pregnancies.

In those days of the early 1960s, however, the couple had friends and parishioners for whom things did not go so well. Some were not able to conceive and had access to no reproductive therapy. Others conceived unintentionally and were faced with an unplanned child in difficult circumstances. Still others felt forced into marriage. Only those with money had safe abortions, and they flew to Japan or Sweden to get them.

The Couple's Reflections

As they look back on their experience of thirty-something years ago, two realizations particularly stand out. First is their largely unquestioned sex-role and family assumptions. In the 1950s, the lines of responsibility and expected behaviors seemed very clear. The second great wave of American feminism had not yet shaken their taken-for-granted views of gender realities.

Thus, *preference* in contraceptive methods was largely his choice, but the *responsibility* for carrying it out was hers. The birthing was *her* event, not *theirs*—it did not dawn on him that he might be present. These assumptions about contraception and birthing were simply the way things were, and it all seemed largely reasonable.

Yet, there were hitches. Since hers was also the major responsibility for infant and child care, he was not even expected to be ready for emergencies. When an emergency came, he was totally unprepared. While this shocked him into more intentional parenting, it was not until years later that he acquired acute awareness of his own "father hunger," hunger for the distant father of his own childhood. Not until then was he viscerally aware of the critical importance of active, nurturant fathering.

The feminist movement has brought enormously important changes in our collective consciousness. Even in a still-sexist society, egalitarian marriages are now sometimes closer to reality. Many women sense their right to bodily self-control and insist on it. We can say thankfully that some men today are also embracing a different view about these things. Yet one of the church's vastly underdeveloped missions is to men—in their desire to look deeply at their own lives and at their cultural masculinity.

Certain cultural expectations about the proper family—its members' roles but also its size—were also very much part of this couple's earlier world. When they shifted their choice from four to two children, they coped with some guilt. Two seemed a bit skimpy when, like Norman Rockwell's *Saturday Evening Post* covers, most of their peers were filling up the station wagons with kids. At least this couple genuinely wanted two. But friends of theirs who wanted none discovered that voluntary childlessness was not a socially respectable option. Today we are more conscious of an overpopulated world, of the cultural relativity of family norms, and of the claims of gender justice. The church can help couples make responsible choices now in ways that seemed unavailable not many years ago.

The couple's second major awareness concerns the vast difference in actual reproductive choices now available one generation later. Part of the difference, of course, is technological. Infertility clinics now have expanded repertoires of therapies, and when infertility persists there are numerous options available besides adoption. Various applications of *in vitro* fertilization, for example, are available to many.

Yet, changed technology is only part of the scene. The actual availability of many reproductive choices depends on social attitudes, political and economic realities, and moral convictions. Since the Supreme Court's opinion in *Griswold* v. *Connecticut* (1965), contraceptive materials have been readily available in all states. Some procedures—artificial insemination and surrogacy, for example—typically require no new technology, but their more frequent use is largely the result of greater social acceptance. The use of artificial insemination by many lesbian couples is relatively new in recent years. So the changes in the reproductive picture are a mix of technological issues and social attitude shifts.

As they reflected about these things, then and now, the couple mused about what it meant. Their theologies told them that technology by itself never solves anything, and that human history is not a smooth ride into a better future. Yet they also wanted to celebrate the genuine advances in reproductive options for many people. Still, those advances were not available to all, nor was their availability, once secured, guaranteed to last. They also knew that "new occasions teach new duties," and the "Who owns the frozen embryos?" type of question would become more and not less frequent in the future.

In some ways it all made them relieved that they were beyond childbearing age. Most of all, however, it made them aware of how important it was to have a community in which to struggle and wonder together about these things. For them the church, in one form or another, was that special community.

IO

Embryos and Ethics:
Old and New Quandaries
About Life's Beginnings

In a recent sermonic commentary on *in vitro* fertilization and
frozen embryos, a leading television evangelist concluded, "God's
way is still the best way." I wholeheartedly agree. How could
any serious Christian conclude otherwise? The theological-
ethical problem, of course, is knowing what God's way is. The
preacher was sure he knew exactly what that was: God's way
meant "natural" sexual reproduction without any assistance
through technological intervention. However, some of us believe
that if we absolutized a noninterventionist principle and bap-
tized everything that occurs "naturally," we would quickly wipe
out most of modern medicine. We doubt that would be in accord
with God's desire for us.

In the usual course of events, infertility problems occur, currently in about 20 percent of American couples of childbearing
age. And in the so-called "unnatural" course of events, we are in
the midst of dramatic developments in reproductive technology.

Sometimes it is difficult to distinguish what is old and what is
new in reproductive interventions. Some practices have been

with us for a long time—for example, mechanical contraception, abortion, sex selection, and sterilization. However, also old is artificial insemination, which has been used for human reproduction for some two hundred years. Still older is surrogate motherhood, a practice dating back thousands of years and exemplified in Abram and Sarai's enlistment of Hagar to resolve the couple's infertility problem (Genesis 16).

Yet some of the old practices now have new twists. Instead of practicing infanticide for sex selection, we can attempt to influence fetal sex through sperm centrifuge. Or we can discover the fetus's sex through amniocentesis or ultrasound and then elect abortion if it is "the wrong sex." In addition there are genuinely new developments: *in vitro* fertilization, embryo transfer, embryo freezing, genetic screening, and genetic surgery. Furthermore, additional techniques are on the horizon: cloning, artificial placentas, alteration of the genetic composition of embryos, and doubtless others. All this range of developments poses both perennial and new issues about life's beginnings and what it means to be human.

How shall we reflect on these things? Dualisms make for bad theology. They also give rise to poor ethics and harmful medical practice. In contrast, an incarnational perspective strives against every splitting of spirit from body, of mind from matter, of men from women, and of human beings from the rest of nature. It attempts to understand persons holistically and to understand spirit as inseparable from matter. It sees human life intended for harmony with the natural environment, not superior to it. Against any hierarchies of superiority and control, it seeks to express our essential human equality. With this perspective in mind, let us look at four issues that give shape to our specific responses to reproductive technologies.

Basic Worldviews

First, our basic worldviews, whatever they may be, will give significant form to our reproductive ethics, just as to any other part of our moral lives. A worldview is our picture of reality, including our assumptions about those ultimate powers that determine our existence, our values about what is most worthful, and our assumptions about human nature and the world in which we live. Until something radically challenges our worldviews, we tend to take them for granted. They just seem self-evidently true. I suggest that the dualisms present in our dominant cultural worldviews have distorted our perspectives in a variety of ways that affect our perspectives on reproductive ethics.

For one thing, our culture exalts the individual consumer. Such a worldview is dualistic, because it splits us from our intimate connections with other people and, indeed, from the earth itself. A consumerist mentality does not take seriously the welfare of the global biosystem or even the welfare of the human species within it. The primary interests are controlling matter in order to consume it and producing high quality consumables for maximum gratification.

When infertility occurs, a consumerist mentality tends to shift the focus away from the prospective child to the potential parents' gratification. Now the desire is not primarily the child for the child's sake. It is the desire for a child for the potential parents' gratification. Granted, the same temptation may be present when there are no infertility problems. However, when infertility is a reality and reproductive interventions seem warranted, there is now also the possibility of enhancing the "quality" of the child. Discriminating consumers desire quality products, free from defects and (in this instance) perhaps even of the "right" sex. Now the future child's rights or needs do not loom large. For example, the child's right to a lineage that could give her or him a secure identity may receive little if any consideration. That question simply does not loom large to a consumerist mentality.

Further, a consumerist worldview is congenial to a eugenic mentality. Eugenics involves the use of reproductive technologies not primarily for infertility therapy, but rather in the search for an improved humanity—"a better human product." Some years ago this eugenic mentality appeared in the creation of the California sperm bank that boasted the sperm of Nobel Prize winners. What was once the hope of every pregnant couple—the hope for a healthy child—can become the conviction of the right to a child who not only is healthy but has bodily and mental excellence.

A technological mentality usually accompanies the eugenic focus. We now have the generation of young adults who were the first to grow up completely in the age of the Pill, in which the triumph of technology over conception seemed real. If now we are convinced that human reproduction can be controlled in its negative (contraceptive) aspects, ought we not also to control reproduction in positive directions through the techniques presently available?

When the primary focus is on technological solutions, certain traditional religious views lose their grip. The 1987 Vatican statement on reproductive technologies counseled couples unsuccessful in their fertility treatments to find their sterility the occasion for other important human services such as adoption, work with the poor, or assistance to children with disabilities.[1] Few couples seem content with that, however. Most studies indicate that far more see their infertility as an immense problem to be conquered through the best technological means. It is not a condition to accept with resignation, nor are energies to be redirected elsewhere. Infertility is viewed as an organic problem with a technological answer. For such couples the typical response is to "do anything, try anything."

A dualistic worldview also encourages a mechanistic and reductionist approach to life. Animal reproduction offers illustrations of this. Recently we have debated the use of the bovine-growth hormone. We have created the four-legged chicken, for greater consumer appeal. We have injected human growth genes into the germline of pigs, causing them to grow twice as fast and to become deformed, partially blind, and arthritic. We are crossing species boundaries at an ever-increasing rate, as scientists insert human genes into animals and animal genes into other animal species and into plants. The cost to animals is seldom measured by those with a mechanistic worldview, for animals are seen just as body-machines. Further, the impact of human reproductive technology used on animal and plant life for commercial gain will take its toll primarily on the world's poor, for significant disruption of agricultural patterns always exacts a heavier toll on those who live closest to the land.

Finally, such a mechanistic perspective can encourage a military mind-set driven by the quest for control and by fear of loss of control. In the recent past, American biological warfare funding increased 700 percent in a space of seven years. We can now quickly manufacture potent pathogens that once were available only in minute quantities. Recombinant DNA techniques can be used for new warfare agents, as genes are programmed into infectious microorganisms to increase their potency.

There are many appropriate uses for reproductive technologies. They are frequently a rich blessing to infertile couples, and our awareness of the temptations that come from cultural and religious dualisms should not bias us against them. However, it is well to begin our reflections with a sober look at the ways that dualistic worldviews can shape our thinking about these things. An open-eyed awareness of our cultural values may be a first step toward wisdom. It can remind us of the invitation to a more sacramental approach which perceives all life as gift and all life as delicately balanced, interrelated, and interdependent.

Sexuality, Marriage, and Parenting

In addition to our basic worldviews, surely our understandings of sexuality, marriage, and parenting affect our approaches to reproductive ethics. One obvious question is this: Is it morally legitimate to separate procreation from marital intercourse? Certainly, most couples have done the reverse for a long time. The widespread acceptance of contraception is proof of this. Most heterosexual couples are completely comfortable making love without any intention of conceiving. In fact, they believe it a moral obligation to *prevent* conception in most of their lovemaking. However, with several reproductive interventions now available, we have begun to ask the question the other way around. We know that we can have sex without procreation. Now we also know that we can have procreation without sex. But *should* we?

Official Roman Catholic teaching has given the clearest response to this question. The Vatican's answer is, no. Since in its view it is never permissible to separate reproduction from marital intercourse, technical interventions such as artificial insemination, *in vitro* fertilization, embryo transfer, and surrogate mothering are forbidden.[2] While the Vatican has been unambiguously clear about this, some individual Catholic moral theologians differ. Richard McCormick, for example, accepts in principle the inseparability of the procreative (baby-making) and unitive (lovemaking) purposes of sex, but believes that not every act of intercourse must hold these together. Rather, he says, "[It is] sufficient that the spheres be held together, so that there is no procreation apart from marriage, and no full sexual intimacy apart from a context of responsibility for procreation."[3] This understanding opens the door to certain reproductive interventions such as *in vitro* fertilization using the husband's sperm.

Jews and Protestants are not all of one mind. Some are close to the Vatican position. Others, myself included, are far more open to reproductive interventions—on the basis of a different theology of sexuality and marriage. About three hundred years ago, some Puritans, Quakers, and Anglicans began to understand and to teach that God's *primary* purpose in establishing marriage and sexuality was not procreation but rather loving companionship. This understanding of the primacy of companionship led to a clear acceptance of birth control, for now acts of sexual love had their own justification quite apart from procreation. Indeed, the Puritans (who were not nearly as antisexual as popular image has made them) had a choice phrase for it. If babies came along, they said, that was "an added blessing"; but babies were not the central purpose of marriage or of sexual intercourse itself.

Dualism tempts us to split the body from the spirit. Thus, it also tempts us to separate sexual *acts* from the *meanings* they have for us. We then end up with a "physicalist" or "intrinsicalist" interpretation of sexual acts, the notion that certain physical acts always mean the same thing and can be defined as intrinsically right or wrong, quite apart from the spirit or meanings they have to the persons. This approach does violence to our wholeness as persons. We are spirited bodies, not just bodies.

The continuing quandary about masturbation is an illustration. This common practice is still laden with awkward silence and guilt, though if we adults were more open and positive in the attitudes we convey to adolescents, there might be fewer teenage pregnancies. In any event, for many persons, partnered as well as single, such self-pleasuring has a valued place in their patterns of sexual expression throughout their adult lives. To them, masturbation does not signal immaturity or self-centeredness, nor does it mean escape from relationship. Rather, it is simply one of their sexual expressions, and one through which they can particularly express certain meanings of bodily self-love.

However, some dualistic religious interpretations believe that masturbation is always and intrinsically wrong. It does not matter what the act may mean to the person. Whether a man masturbates to avoid relating sexually to his wife or whether he masturbates to produce semen for their *in vitro* fertilization, the act is still believed wrong. The body has its intrinsic meanings quite apart from spirit. A holistic body theology, on the other hand, insists that sexual acts are not good or bad in and of themselves. You cannot judge a book by its cover or an act by its physical contours. It all depends on the interaction of the physical expression with its relational meanings to the persons affected by those acts—body and spirit together. It would seem likely that masturbation for purposes of *in vitro* fertilization (IVF) is usually an act of faith, hope, and love; it is hardly deserving of negative evaluation.

A related question frequently raised is this: Is conception in a laboratory petri dish intrinsically wrong? Again, the answer from a holistic bodyself perspective must be no. The morality of procreative actions, whether done in bedroom or laboratory, cannot be neatly cataloged by their physical contours. The appropriateness of such acts must be judged by their relational meanings as well as the physical expressions. The basic question is, How do our bodily actions and the meanings we believe them to have fit into the overall meaning and good of this relationship and this wider community of life?

I do not see the separation of procreation from loving sexual intercourse as ideal. It would be ideal if we did not need any reproductive technologies. It would be ideal if every couple who truly desired children and were prepared for parenting could have them. We are not living in a perfect world, however. So the question is, in this less-than-ideal world where unwanted infertilities occur, What is our responsible action? In many situations IVF can be an act of deep faithfulness and participation in God's creative activity. Now we come to a stickier question: What about third-party involvements? What about sperm donors, or

egg donors, or surrogate mothers? Some theologians label all
these tactics as adultery. I do not. Adultery is not essentially a
biological question. It cannot be defined simply by bodily actions
apart from the spirit. It is not essentially the intrusion of a third
party's body or body products into the marital dyad. The adultery question has arisen in reproductive ethics because, for
example, some have labeled the use of donor sperm in artificial
insemination adulterous since it violates a married couple's
rightful physical monopoly of each other's sexual organs. Again,
that way of perceiving the issue is dualistic. It splits body from
spirit by defining adultery simply as a physiological matter.

Adultery, more adequately understood, is the willful and
harmful violation (adulteration) of the primacy, the perma-
nence, and the honesty of the marriage. Thus, some extramarital
relationships that involve no physical sexual expression whatever can still be adulterous. On the other hand, certain physical
acts that introduce a third person's sexuality into the marriage
may not be adulterous at all. There are, to be sure, risks
in introducing a third party. However, if we hold together the
realm of meanings and intentions, on the one hand, and the
realm of physical acts, on the other, I do not see how the participation of a third party *in principle* constitutes adultery. In
many situations, the participation of a third party might well be
an expression of the couple's profound marital fidelity. It all
depends.

There are other questions. Do an infertile couple have the
absolute and inviolable right to produce children if they so
desire? Ethical questions are always finally theological ones, and
so it is with "rights." My conviction is that there are no absolute
rights of any sort. Only God is absolute. Everything else is
relative. The right of the infertile couple to reproduce with
medical assistance is related to other factors. What are some of
them?

The couple's readiness for parenting is one. What about the
larger social question of spending scarce medical resources for
infertility therapy when the planet is already overcrowded? This
important question is relevant to the whole society and not just
to the infertile couple. Fairness requires that fertile people not
demand that only those persons who experience infertility be

responsible for dealing with scarce resources and overpopulation. If couples should restrict their reproduction because of such social concerns (which they should), then that means everyone equally, and not just those struggling with fertility problems.

What about gay couples, lesbian couples, or unwed heterosexual couples? Should they be allowed access to assisted reproduction? Again, the question cannot be answered in the abstract. Many such couples would make, and do make, excellent parents. That we know. The moral question drives us back to the theological one: What really constitutes a marriage?

According to the weight of both Christian and Jewish traditions, marriage is not constituted by the combination of legal permission (a license) and a wedding ceremony. Rather, a marriage is created by a faithful, enduring covenant between the partners. Important though laws and ceremonies may be, they do not create marriages, but rather they recognize and celebrate covenants that are essentially constituted by love and not by law. I do not minimize the possibility of complicating social factors for the child born of a nontraditional union. Such factors always ought to be assessed. However, what is centrally at stake is the security, stability, and strength of the partners' covenant—that is the core stuff of marriage and the core requisite for parenthood.

This approach does not endorse utter permissiveness in these things. I do not suggest that if the technological means are available, their use is necessarily appropriate. We know from human experience that children tend to fare better when they are clear about their lineage and when their family unit is recognized by others as stable and valid. Again, at the core of it all is love. Durable, dependable, warm, life-giving parental love is what the child needs most. A monopoly on such love has never been held by legally wed heterosexuals.

Regarding these issues of sexuality, marriage, and parenting, exceptionless, absolute ethical norms are impossible. Only God is absolute. That does not mean we are left without significant guidelines. It does mean that we take seriously a whole series of concrete realities: the stability, love, and justice of relationships; the potential good for children who may be born; the networks of supportive communities; and our desires for the wholeness God intends for us. On such things "it all depends."

Embryos and Personhood

Now let us turn to a third issue: embryos and personhood. First, a brief note on language: while there are rightful biological distinctions between the zygote, the blastocyst, and the embryo, in discussions such as these the term "embryo" is typically used to include all these stages of the developing human organism in its earliest weeks of life. I will adopt that usage.

Several major questions cluster around the status of the embryo. In IVF procedures, is it right to destroy unneeded embryos, or is such destruction tantamount to abortion? What about research on embryos? Or their freezing and storage? Or their commercial sale by an embryo bank? Each of these different questions hinges centrally on the meaning and value of embryonic life.

One ethical position holds that the embryo is a person in the full moral sense of that word, deserving of all personal legal and moral rights. This supposition is defended in several different ways. Some argue it on the basis of the embryo's unique genetic composition. Others maintain that the embryo's *potentiality* for becoming a full person means in fact that it is *actually* a person. Still others claim that drawing the line of personhood any time after conception is just too arbitrary, so we must begin to treat life from the moment of conception as personhood.

I am not fully persuaded by any of these arguments. Yes, the embryo has a unique genetic composition. And it is genetically unique *human* life—it is not a sparrow or a pig. However, each individual sparrow or pig is also genetically unique, so it is not simply genetic uniqueness as such that is at stake. We make some moral distinctions between these creatures and the creatures we call human persons. Our reasoning about this is necessarily somewhat circular: we call "human" what we recognize as "human" and "person" what we recognize as "person." We reserve the language of "the human person" for that life with those qualities of consciousness, self-awareness, memory, and capacities for social interaction that we recognize as distinctly human and personal qualities. Further, if one argues that potentiality itself constitutes personhood, one could push that argument back to claiming full personal rights for human sperm cells and unfertilized human eggs. They too are potentially persons, if the right things happen at the right time. Yet I suspect that few would argue that case. That kind of "potentiality" stretches the imagination too far if it is taken as "actuality."

Some will say that the embryo's *gradual* development into personal capacities makes the drawing of any lines after conception just too arbitrary. The fact that this development is an ongoing continuum without sharp breaks makes distinctions simply too fuzzy. Yet "fuzzy" is the way life is. To say that it is sometimes difficult to distinguish between a man who is bald and one who is not bald is true, and my own thinning hair demonstrates the ambiguity well. That, however, does not mean that there is no difference. It just means (quite literally in this case!) that things do get fuzzy sometimes. When that happens, what we name those realities should show our respect for them and our concern about what such naming will mean for all who are affected. To say we cannot be precise about the moment when human life must be treated as personal is true. That is one thing. To say that there is no relevant moral difference between a fertilized egg and a late-stage human fetus is quite another.

We must live with ambiguity here. With embryos we are dealing with the earliest prepersonal forms of human life. They deserve our respect. That respect and care should grow as personal potentiality grows. To discard unneeded embryos in an IVF procedure is not the killing of persons. Neither should the discarding be done without our awareness that here we are deliberately sacrificing something of real human value in favor of what we believe is a still greater human value. In this case we justify discarding unneeded embryos because of the greater value with which we hold the mother's safety—to implant multiple embryos poses predictable risks to her. We justify the destruction of the embryos because we hold in even greater value the future birthing of a person who would not exist apart from the IVF process.

Still, there is something of the morally tragic in this procedure that we ought not to forget. We are consenting to the sacrifice of a form of human life. That reminder need not paralyze us or prevent the responsible use of IVF, of which there may well be many applications. It is simply, and importantly, a reminder that our consciences must never be dulled, even when we choose the greater value.

There are extraordinary moral ironies here. To avoid religious criticisms about embryo destruction, some IVF clinics now refuse to destroy any fertilized eggs, implanting all of them into the woman. Such a practice, however, like the refusal to allow early-stage abortions, risks significant dangers to fully developed persons—women. In short, it values embryonic life over personal life.

Another irony appears with the question of research on embryos. In recent years a widely publicized Tennessee court case involved contested frozen embryos. A couple, having unsuccessfully tried IVF for years, ended up with seven embryos frozen in liquid nitrogen. Then came a marital separation and a dispute over custody of the embryos. The woman wanted them because, even if single, she wanted to be a mother. The man wanted to control the embryos because, now separated, he did not want to be a father. Many commentators said that this was the quintessential case of technology outrunning ethics. But it was not. For years ethicists and legal scholars have been warning that we need federal policies for dealing with research on and preservation of embryos, but the government has been timid. For years the federal government has banned funding for research on IVF. Our scientists simply do not understand infertility very well, and without public money for better research, we are left with a dilemma. Since the failure rate is exceedingly high, doctors remove more eggs and try to fertilize more than will be used. Then, having no legal guidance on what to do with unneeded embryos, rather than risk their destruction they implant them or freeze them. Thus, we have created a situation in which thousands of unneeded embryos are brought into being, many of which are destroyed simply in the thawing and many others of which are kept frozen because we do not know what to do with them.

The strange irony here is that a physicalist, nonincarnational understanding of embryonic life is causing more risk to and destruction of the very embryos we need to respect. Embryos are not simply the same as another piece of tissue. Nor are they "little children" (as the Tennessee judge finally decreed). Personal life involves at the very least the capacity for sentience, the awareness and feeling of sensations, pleasure and pain—which no scientist I know of seriously attributes to embryos. A holistic, incarnational understanding of personal life as union of body and spirit will not automatically resolve all these difficult issues. Yet it will significantly help us to sort out some of the differences in the values we attribute to the forms of human life and the protections we must assign to them.

The Moral Status of Women

The final issue for comment is the moral status of women—the ways that women are understood and treated in reproductive interventions. A dualistic worldview not only splits body from spirit, but also subordinates women to men. How is this reflected in reproductive issues?

First, the physical and emotional risks in reproductive interventions are typically much greater for women than for men. The technologies we currently have are more bodily and emotionally invasive to women, and hence more ethically problematic for them.

In one sense, of course, the physical risks appear to be inescapably biological. In IVF, compared to the man's simple (and probably pleasurable) process of securing his semen for donation, the removal of eggs from the woman is a complicated surgical procedure. Other procedures are no less complex. Embryo transfer is a fairly elaborate and physically invasive procedure. Amniocentesis has its own risks. And, of course, a surrogate mother carries all the usual physical risks of pregnancy.

Even though with our present medical knowledge we do not know how to do these reproductive techniques with less invasiveness to women, it should give every man pause to know that all of this is still done by a largely male-controlled research science and medical establishment. In a patriarchal society (which is still largely with us) men, even without consciousness of the fact, likely will accept risks to women more readily than they will accept risks to themselves or other men.

In addition to bodily risk and invasiveness, there are perils of the spirit in certain reproductive interventions. Surrogate pregnancies dramatically illustrate the danger of exploiting women. Surrogates usually need the money and are contracted by more affluent couples. Typically they are paid a fee for their nine months of pregnancy and potential emotional complications, a fee often no larger than that paid to the (usually male) attorney who makes the arrangement. Exploitation is not the same as coercion. Granted, the surrogate may not feel coerced. She may enjoy much of the pregnancy experience, she may want to help others, and, needing the money, she may choose this option over others less desirable to her. The fact, however, is that women in need of money are still selling the use of their bodies. That is always a risk to human dignity. I do not believe that surrogacy is morally the same as prostitution. They are quite different things. On the other hand, neither do I believe that surrogacy can be compared fairly to other risky occupations that we willingly allow others to choose—occupations such as coal mining or race-car driving. Nor is surrogacy equitably compared to selling a pint of blood or an ejaculate of semen. In bodily and personal investment it would seem more comparable to selling a kidney.

In significant ways, the emotional risks to the surrogate seem unpredictable. Her anonymity is usually impossible, for she almost always knows the biological father. To a degree unmatched by the contracting couple, she experiences psychological bonding with the developing life in her uterus and, as we have seen in more than one publicized case, she may not be able to predict the emotional complications of separation from her biological child. Nor are potential side effects on the surrogate's other children neatly predictable. In these various ways surrogacy cannot fairly be compared to the risks of adoption. In our adoption procedures we do not ask women to bear children intentionally for the purpose of offering them for adoption; rather, we use adoption as a creative response to the sad predicament of the unwanted child.

Nevertheless, it is not fair to picture surrogacy as a practice that simply reduces certain women to baby-making machines for wealthier consumers. The risks of exploiting a woman in both body and spirit are surely there. Yet legal prohibitions of the practice bring other dualistic risks. Laws that completely prohibit surrogacy may well be one more form of paternalistic restriction on the reproductive choices of women, and we have had too much of that. If women need protection from exploitation, women also deserve to have their autonomy respected and their reproductive choices protected. Perhaps our better wisdom lies in public regulation that would include screening and counseling of potential surrogate mothers and that would require a waiting period after birth (a waiting period comparable to the usual practice in ordinary adoptions). Without destroying the woman's reproductive and bodily freedom, perhaps such measures would help protect some women from needless exploitation and others from making irrevocable and regrettable choices. In any event, women's voices should be finally determinative in the shaping of such public policy.[4]

Issues regarding women in reproductive ethics, like those of embryos and personhood, sexuality and parenting, and even our basic worldviews, pose complex ethical questions that often cannot be tidily resolved. Our search for wise practice and fair public policies will be served best when we hold before ourselves an incarnational vision of human wholeness.

Should We Because We Can?

A story from ancient Greece tells of the man of great intellect and courage who was revered for saving his city from enemy warriors. But something was wrong in the city: a plague had fallen on its fertility. Infertility afflicted plants and animals as well as the people. The man confidently promised to discover the causes of the plague and restore fertility to the city. Resolutely he set to work, raging against the representatives of caution, leaving no stone unturned, no possibility untried. He solved the problem, but in the process made visible all the dark details of his own origins and ruined his own life and his family's. In the end, he learned too late the price of overconfidence, of overweening desire to control his own fate. In a symbolic rejection of his desire to see everything, he inflicted blindness on himself.

This is Sophocles's story of Oedipus, a tragic figure who finally had to learn his limits through suffering. Is that our fate?

Who is Oedipus? The Greek chorus calls him a paradigm of "man." In a sense different than the chorus intended, that seems true. Oedipus represents not humanity so much as that form of distorted masculinity that prizes mastery and control as supreme goods. Such an image of humanity, indeed, has affected much of our technology and science. It is time to move beyond mastery and control into visions of participation and harmony. These visions are becoming even more important as reproductive technologies grow more sophisticated and their use more widespread. The question inevitably is framed: Should we, simply because we can?

It seems obvious to say that we should not do everything we can. To answer yes would invite "the capacity fallacy"—if we have the capacity to do it, we ought to do it. Yet some scientists believe precisely that. They will say that scientists have the moral right to do whatever they have the technical capacity to do because new knowledge is intrinsically valuable, the right to knowledge is a basic human liberty, and scientific progress is necessary to control our future.

When we move from reproductive issues to other kinds of technologies, however, the error is obvious. We do have the nuclear capacity to decimate global life, but we know that we ought not to do it. Indeed, some of us think that we ought not even to retain that technology in our possession.

Almost instinctively, we sense that there are limits on exercising our scientific muscle. Those are the moral limits imposed by a religious sensitivity about life and the sacramental web of creation. Such sensitivities are not limited to any particular religious groups. In fact, many who claim no organized religion show more reverence for creation than many who do. What is needed is a moral sensitivity that is clear about using our scientific capacities fully for—*but only for*—enhancing the value and meaning of life as it has been given to us by that holy, mysterious, creative power that is within and infinitely beyond us.

Thus, there are limits to what we ought to do in genetic manipulations. There are limits to our virtue and wisdom in knowing what perfect human beings ought to look like. There are boundaries in creation itself that wisdom bids us respect.

There is yet another fallacy, one often called "the inevitability fallacy." Its reasoning is that science and technology build their own momentum and we will *in fact* inevitably use whatever technologies we develop. So, it is argued, if we develop the capacity to grow human embryos in the laboratory beyond the blastocyst stage, it is inevitable that someday we will extend this to full-term ectogenesis, developing infants in the laboratory, from conception to full term. Or we will in fact alter the cellular composition of embryos with precise genetic manipulations to produce our desired design of human life. Or we will in fact develop commercial embryo banks where couples or individuals might shop for the product of their choice.

Will we? The argument that one thing inevitably leads to another, and before you know it we have undesirable (and sometimes unforeseen) results—that argument is variously called "the slippery slope" or "the wedge argument" or "the camel's nose." There are actually two different forms of this argument, and distinguishing them is useful. One deals with the logic of justification, and the other with social prediction.

The logical argument says that if you approve of step A, then you have approved steps B, C, and D if they follow from the same basic principle. Consider some familiar arguments about terminal illness, for example. Some will say that if you allow A, the withdrawal of fluids and nutrition from dying patients, soon you move to B, killing them directly, and then shortly you will embrace C, killing "undesirables" in nursing homes. The question for good ethics is this: Are we clear about our principles? Can we articulate them and stand by them? And can we know that what justifies practice A does not in any way justify B or C?

In this case, making the dying process more humane for the dying does not justify actively killing them. In the first case (A), the disease is the agent of death and we are just acknowledging that it is no longer appropriate to continue our resistance to the inevitable, because of the suffering that is being prolonged. That principle does not justify either B, active killing of the dying, or C, killing those who are not dying but whose lives have become burdensome to others. The latter two simply do not follow from the former.

Move back now to reproduction. We need to know much more than we currently do about the causes of infertility. If we knew more, we would not have to put the infertile through such expensive, emotionally taxing, and often ineffective procedures. If we knew more, we would not have to fertilize so many eggs in IVF. Thus, we want to learn as much as we can about the processes of fertilization, growth, implantation, and differentiation of human embryos. This seems justified, and its principle does not lead to other things we might abhor. Our principle in this example might be: *Carefully regulated research on embryos is justified, but only to promote effective therapy for those involuntarily infertile.*

Pay attention to what is said and what is not said in that principle. It is *carefully regulated* research, not "anything goes." It is for assistance in cases of *involuntary* infertility, not for the simple convenience of a couple who do not wish to go through pregnancy. It is for *therapeutic* purposes, not for discovering means of genetic manipulation to produce "a better child."

Thus, clarity about the logic of our principles is imperative. But will this answer the second kind of slippery-slope argument? That argument contends that when we create a certain technology, the momentum of social conditions and history will sooner or later inevitably lead to its use, regardless of our good principles.

It all depends. There is nothing fated about it. In no small measure it depends on pastors, chaplains, nurses, doctors, social workers, therapists, counselors, community leaders, and informed members of the public. In no small measure it depends on those voluntary associations that stimulate and sustain the ethical dialogue among us—including, we hope, the churches significantly among them.

Ethics is an inexact science. Indeed, it is more like art than science. As with art, it is never a paint-by-numbers operation. The canvas has no such neat outcomes laid before us. Good ethics, like good art, means knowing *where* to draw the lines and *why*. We are faced with drawing the lines concerning what constitutes legitimate therapy—treatment of the genuine *needs* of persons and not simply their *desires*. These distinctions are not always obvious or neat, but struggle with them we must. Thus, I believe that there are significant moral differences, for example, between:

- respecting the desire of many women for motherhood, on the one hand, and promoting an ideology of motherhood as the ultimate goal of all "normal" women, on the other;
- abortion when serious genetic defect is discovered and abortion when, on the other hand, "the wrong sex" is discovered;

- IVF for infertility therapy, and IVF combined with surrogacy for a couple's convenience;
- technologies that realistically promise positive therapy and those whose success rate is so low that they greatly aggravate the emotional and social problems felt by the involuntarily childless;
- those processes which emphasize genetic lineage for the prospective child's well-being and a preoccupation with lineage for inheritance, succession, and paternity;
- those technologies which manipulate women and their bodies as expendable commodities, and those which respect, fulfill, and empower women.

Drawing the lines is what the process is about. We have not always done well in stopping the slippery slope in some areas of our common lives. Our foreign policy and ecological records are particularly blighted in this respect. In medical treatment and research, however, the record has been significantly better. We have often found ways to draw the lines and stop medical processes that showed dehumanizing results. As reproductive technological possibilities multiply, the imperative seems clear: that we persevere in the process of dialogue, careful discernment, and the shaping of a medical and public ethos that respects and nourishes whole persons in a sacramental world.

I I

Illness as Body Interpretation: HIV and AIDS

One particular disease in our time poses a profound challenge to body theology: the HIV virus and AIDS. The focus for body theology, however, is not on the disease as such, but on the illness. As we have seen in chapter 8, disease is the organic reality. With AIDS it is the process of a virus attacking and destroying the body's immune system, rendering the person susceptible to a host of opportunistic infections. Illness, on the other hand, is how we understand the meanings of this organic process for persons. Illness equals disease plus social interpretation.

Let us recall the now-familiar meaning patterns commonly associated with AIDS:

- It has linked together in one fearful combination the two greatest anxieties of our society: sex and death.
- It has thus far primarily struck those who have already been interpreted as bearing social stigma and who have thus been marginalized.
- It has been moralized in ways that have blamed the one with the disease.

- It is a disease for which we at present must rely heavily on prevention education, and yet such education has met public resistance precisely because it appears to condone socially disapproved activities.
- It is a disease spread by sexual fluids and blood, which are the very symbols of life itself and which are the potent reminders of our interconnectedness and vulnerability.

In a very real way, to understand AIDS is to understand ourselves personally confronting the issues of mortality, sexuality, our relationships, and our communities. With this in mind, let us first consider the societal interpretations of AIDS and how some affected persons themselves interpret the disease.

Metaphors are the necessary focus for considering the societal interpretations of AIDS. Throughout history people have used metaphors to interpret the human body. The apostle Paul called the body a temple. To Descartes and Newton the body was a machine. The list of body metaphors in literature is long.

Susan Sontag reminds us that we use metaphors not only for the body itself but also for bodily diseases.[1] In the nineteenth century it was tuberculosis—so intractable, capricious, and mysterious—that was particularly laden with the trappings of metaphor, and in the twentieth century it became cancer. These diseases not only meant a death sentence, but also were felt to be obscene, somehow marking, shaming, and stigmatizing those afflicted. Now AIDS has supplanted these in its metaphorical powers.

We use metaphors not only for diseases but also for epidemics. Here military images are common. Early in this century we talked of the wars against syphilis and tuberculosis, more recently of the war against cancer, and now the war against AIDS. The warfare metaphor reminds us of the invasion by alien forces, of the mobilization of society's resources to repel the enemy, of issues of guilt and innocence—all common things in war, now associated with the spread of a disease.

Early in the epidemic, certain metaphors for AIDS quickly emerged in the media: AIDS as death, AIDS as punishment, AIDS as crime, AIDS as otherness (a means of dividing the world dualistically into "us" and "them").[2] AIDS was also imaged as leprosy, and persons with AIDS quickly became the biblical lepers of our time, quite literally the untouchables.

However, "the plague" rather quickly became the chief metaphor for the disease.[3] And what are the common meanings associated with a plague—now metaphorically connected to AIDS? A plague is an enormous collective calamity, evil, and scourge. AIDS has been seen this way. It is an invasion of the whole society. Moreover, a plague is an alien invasion. White racism early focused social attention on AIDS's alien origins in "dark Africa," coming to North America through black Haiti. A plague punishes a whole society as well as visiting retribution on the individual who contracts it. Note here the difference between AIDS and influenza. Influenza killed twenty million people in our century, but was neither moralized as punishment nor commonly depicted as a plague. In quite a different way, the American right wing has interpreted AIDS as the punishment of the whole society for its decline because of liberal permissiveness. Thus, a nationally known political figure asked whether America had become a country where classroom discussion of the Ten Commandments was impermissible but teacher instructions in safe sodomy were to be mandatory.

The plague metaphor, moreover, encourages us to fear all things bodily. AIDS teaches us to fear sexuality itself. It teaches us to suspect that modern medicine, contrary to our expectations, has not made our bodies safe after all. It teaches us to fear bodily polluting fluids—not only sexual fluids but also contaminated blood and the contaminated Communion cup. Finally, the image of the plague nurtures apocalyptic thinking. To fears of nuclear and ecological catastrophe we now add AIDS, a disease that personalizes the apocalypse in ways that some of these other forces do not.

As it conveys all these meanings, the plague metaphor does something else. It also conveys certain physiological perceptions associated with historic plagues—easy and casual transmission, the need for quarantine and isolation, and death coming quickly after exposure. Yet all of these are inaccurate perceptions when applied to AIDS.

Metaphor permits and even encourages us to give a disease a *moral* meaning. The moral meanings conveyed by society's metaphors for AIDS have not altered the physiology of *pain* for those with the disease. Yet those meanings have enormously increased their emotional *suffering* and the suffering of those close to them. The most prevalent AIDS metaphors all have one common result: they mark the bodily realities of persons with AIDS, and of persons with HIV infection, and of persons labeled as members of "high risk groups" (whether or not they engage in high risk behaviors) in ways that separate them from the rest of the human community. The metaphors say: "You do not belong."

The Person with HIV/AIDS

Now, faced with these powerful social interpretations of AIDS, what might an individual contracting the disease typically experience? What is the course of the suffering, not just the pain? Here I focus on the experience of gay and bisexual males, who in the first years of the epidemic were by far the largest affected group in the United States. Though the epidemiological picture is now changing, gay and bisexual males still comprise the largest numbers of those with HIV and AIDS in all but a few urban areas. (Because of this focus, I will use only the masculine pronouns in the descriptions to follow.)

When faced with the HIV diagnosis, the person first may experience some "psychic numbing" and denial.[4] When he gradually accepts the reality of the diagnosis, he is faced with the necessity of its interpretation. At one level, he "personalizes" the disease, connecting it to the distinctive features of his own life: what does AIDS now mean to his job situation, his family, his personal relationships, his resources? Such personalizing typically brings deep reactions of grief and loss: it feels as though he is losing just about everything, life included. Typically there is anxiety and guilt: about the possibility of having infected someone else, about the suffering that his disease will mean to others, and guilt from the cultural stigmas associated with AIDS. Now he is doubly stigmatized: he is gay and he is infected. All of this has become very personal.

AIDS still occupies what Victor Turner calls a "liminal" space in our social fabric.[5] In other words, its collective meaning is ambiguous. It is still relatively new to us. It is also different from what we have previously experienced with other diseases. It falls between the cracks. The disease and people with it do not fit neatly into our customary categories.[6] Not only is this disease liminal, but so is the person who has it. He is ambiguous both to himself and to others. His illness in many respects is still medically unpredictable, and though given a medical diagnosis, society's unclarity about AIDS makes it difficult for him to get a clear sense of his new role and behavioral expectations.

Yet this liminality itself offers him some room to "play with" and construct the meanings that the disease has for him. His body now has AIDS. And if his body has it, he has it. So what does that mean now and what will that mean to him during the rest of his days?

If and when the HIV infection develops into AIDS, his body begins to carry the signs of the disease. He is branded—once as gay, now twice stigmatized. He is symbolically associated with a plague that brings contagion and mass death. He becomes accustomed to rejection, both overt and subtle. He needs care and nurturance, yet may suspect the motives of those who give it.

In the face of these threats, he tries to protect himself from others who would brand him with a tainted identity. For a time he might try to remain socially invisible and pass as normal. When the disease makes passing no longer possible, he may isolate and insulate himself from all except a small, safe number of personal contacts. He may try to distance himself physically from others who have the disease, to protect himself from the constant reminders they bear. Or he may distance himself psychically by defining AIDS more as a social problem than as his own personal issue.

Finally, and significantly, he comes to a point where he must either continue with endless avoidance or embrace the disease. He can embrace AIDS by taking it into the very center of his personal identity, integrating in a deep way this new body reality into his selfhood.

Many do this through involvement in AIDS support groups, which become a central focus for their identities and where shame and isolation give way to a collective identification. Some are able to construct very positive self-images, proud that they are not victims dying with AIDS but rather persons living with

AIDS. Some actually find new opportunities for social affirmation, sometimes through affirmations not previously experienced, as they carry out community education and leadership tasks in AIDS prevention and care. Some find that the disease has reawakened their creative energies in such mediums as writing, painting, and photography. For some, embracing the disease takes on ideological or spiritual dimensions. One man says, "At first I saw it only as a curse; now I see it as a blessing." Others testify that the disease has helped them to ask important life questions and to realize growth they would not otherwise have had. Another says, "I never before in my life felt like I belonged here. For the most part, I felt like I was stranded on a hostile planet—I didn't know why. But now with the disease and what I've learned in my life, I feel like I really have something by which I can help other people."[7]

This integration of the disease into the self can mean a significant reconnection of body and self. For some it may bring a sense of empowerment even in the midst of increasing physical affliction. One man with AIDS writes of seeing an acquaintance at a Gay Pride festival: "He was looking good, still well-muscled and happy—proudly showing his body off despite an extensive case of Kaposi's Sarcoma lesions marking his back and face."[8]

The past decade has produced ample testimony that many with AIDS have been able to name the meanings of their disease in empowering and reintegrating ways. They have discovered greater connectedness with the larger body of life. In the midst of society's destructive metaphorical interpretations of AIDS, that this should be possible at all—for at least some persons—is cause for wonder. Christianly perceived, it is a miraculous resurrection—yes, even a resurrection of the body.

Whatever their response, however, persons with AIDS dramatically illustrate both the inevitability and the significance of what is often less evident to the rest of us. All of us constantly are faced with the task of interpreting and giving meaning to our bodies. Disease makes us acutely aware of what is, in less dramatic circumstances, a seldom-conscious process. The more serious the disease and the more heavily laden with social metaphor, the more crucial the interpretation will be for the quality of our lives.

To a medical profession heavily shaped by Aesculapian and Cartesian understandings, the patient's illness—the interpretations—often seems quite secondary to the organic disease. Nevertheless, particularly when that disease is socially stigmatized and has no cure, the patient's meanings may be at least as important as medical interventions in dealing with suffering and the quality of life. In many ways this is true also for those of us whose responsibility it may be to care for persons living with AIDS. To the caregivers we now turn.

The Caregivers in AIDS

Socrates taught us that one of the most important admonitions for good ethics is "Know thyself." To do so is not always easy. At times we might feel like the nineteenth-century philosopher Schopenhauer. As legend has it, one day he was wandering in a Berlin park contemplating the deep problems of existence when a policeman, taking him for a vagrant, accosted him with "Who are you, and what are you doing here?" The philosopher shook his head and replied, "I wish I knew. I wish I knew."

However impossible it is to know ourselves completely, some insightful self-understanding is always ethically critical. Our decisions and actions inevitably will be shaped by who we are. For AIDS caregivers, that self-knowledge may be both pivotal and particularly difficult because of the very nature of the disease and its interpretation in our time. Those presently giving the greatest amount of continued care to persons with AIDS usually are not medical professionals. One reason for this is that during lengthy periods of the disease the person with it can be cared for outside a hospital or other institutional setting. Another reason, however, relates not so much to the disease as to the illness. Negative interpretations held by many medical professionals limit their willingness to become involved. A recent survey by the American Medical Association discovered that nearly one third of primary-care physicians feel no responsibility to treat persons with AIDS. Further, more than a third of the internists and family practitioners reported that they would feel "nervous" around homosexual people and view homosexuality as "a threat to many of our basic social institutions."[9]

In the paragraphs that follow I want to address rather personally those readers who have elected to invest themselves in giving direct care to persons with AIDS. Other readers not involved in these particular ways may find insight for themselves by, for the moment, placing themselves in the caregiver's situation.

What are the shaping realities that a person brings to any moral situation? How might these be understood with reference to the AIDS caregiver? I want to suggest six.

First, we bring *the stories of our own moral experience*. While this seems self-evident, it needs to be named. Whenever I listen to AIDS caregivers I hear powerful stories. I hear stories of caring and compassion, of grief and anger, of commitment to justice. I hear stories describing stress, tiredness, aching sadness, and bereavement overload. I also hear stories that acknowledge unresolved issues from other relationships, issues now being played out in AIDS caregiving. To say that our own stories—including all our formative experiences past and present quite apart from our actual caregiving—play into the ways we respond to AIDS situations is to say the obvious. Even so, recognition of the obvious is important, for only then can we get some self-critical distance on our own lives so that we might better understand what is happening now and how we might respond more effectively. The more self-aware I am, the better I can relate my own story to the story of the person with AIDS. I will know more clearly where I end and where he or she begins, where my own feelings and experiences are useful for the other and where they (though utterly real and important to me) are something to handle in other ways. "Know thyself and thine own story."

Second, we bring *our values*. Obviously these also shape our decisions and actions. Individuals become involved in AIDS caregiving because of what they value. They value people and their inherent worth. They value compassion and justice. Such values are part of their character.

Our values do not always harmonize neatly, however, and ethical dilemmas arise as we experience conflict in our internalized values. A little introspection, for example, tells us that the reasons we have gotten involved in AIDS caregiving are quite mixed. Yes, we have been moved to action by compassion and justice. But we also value our own self-interest, our images of ourselves as decent people, and the good opinions that others might have of us. The values that brought us into the AIDS situation in the first place are not neatly harmonious. Once involved, we find more value conflict. For example, we may be committed to the values of self-determination and relief of suffering, on the one hand, and the value of life preservation on the other. Yet in particular AIDS situations these values do not all seem realizable. Hence, the person for whom we care begins to speak of suicide, and the conflict within us is acute.

Something now obvious needs to be underscored: our value conflicts are *not just out there* somewhere. They are *in here*. When I have a dilemma, I do not just have a value conflict that is somehow external to me. I am a *conflicted self*. When that is the case, it is the better part of ethical wisdom to name it. Then, when we adjudicate our conflicting values, we will know what parts of *ourselves* we have chosen to suppress. We will know better the ambiguous selfhood with which we have chosen to live. "Know thyself and thy values"—even when, and especially when, they are in conflict.

Third, we bring *our various roles and relationships* into our caregiving.[10] These also give shape to our responses. A role is simply a cluster of expectations that others have for our behaviors in certain relationships. Thus, AIDS caregivers "play" certain roles. Certain things are expected of them, and those expectations influence their decisions and actions. Yet the caregivers always have other roles in addition to their work with persons with AIDS. They have family roles, community roles, other professional roles. These clusters of expectations do not always mesh well.

Any time we experience role conflict, we experience stress. Ordinarily, we are able to adjust our role conflicts to reduce that stress to manageable proportions. But AIDS is not ordinary. AIDS caregiving can be imperialistic, intruding on our other roles, and there seems little we can do about this if we are to hang in there with persons whose needs keep increasing with time. If you are a volunteer caregiver, your job may suffer. If you are a professional in AIDS care, your family roles may suffer. The caregiving role can become a powerful center around which other roles come to be organized. Your own coping skills, your own informal support networks, become crucial for your own self-care. Again, then, we have the counsel, "Know thyself." Know and name the role stresses that you bring to the ethical dilemmas of AIDS, for then your decisions will be wiser.

Fourth, we bring *our worldviews,* which give shape to our decisions too. For some of us, these are religious worldviews— perceptions of the world that are shaped by our religious convictions. For others of us little formal religiosity is involved. Nevertheless, all of us have worldviews—certain convictions and images concerning what we value most, what it all means, what people are like, what life means, and where it is all going.

Think, for example, of a particular religious worldview. Some of us have learned to view human nature in certain ways, believing that we are all created in the image of God: there is a fineness, an enormous worth, a grandeur about every person (including ourselves). Some of us also see people (ourselves included) as sinners as well: we are insecure and prone to twist situations toward our own self-interest. People are finite: we are limited, we are not gods; we are human, and we cannot do everything. When we stir all these convictions together, we grasp something of the paradoxical complexity of our humanity.

To make one application, when you are carrying heavy stress because of the enormous needs of an AIDS situation, remember that you (as well as everyone else) are a person of fineness and great worth. Also remember that you (and others too) are a sinner. Others may make unrealistic demands on you, and you may respond out of your own insecurities and need for approval. Remember that we are not gods. We will be more effective and we will make wiser decisions when we know that we cannot do it all. In short, whatever your fundamental beliefs about people and life's meanings, you will carry all of that into your ethical decisions. "Know thyself," and know what your worldview does to shape you and your actions.

If our stories, our values, our roles, and our worldviews give shape to us and to our ethics, so also, in the fifth place, do *our fears.* Among the diseases most of us have in some way experienced, AIDS stands in a class by itself in its power to evoke fears. Its relentless spread to more and more persons of color and to the marginalized poor may evoke our own unresolved anxieties about race and class. The fact that it is still incurable, in a time when we have come to expect modern medicine to cure every contagious disease, evokes our fear that maybe medicine has not made our bodies safe after all. Its links with blood contagion can evoke primitive fears of bad blood—not only in blood banks, but symbolically in contaminated Communion cups. Though we cognitively know the impossibility of casual transmission, subterranean fears might still linger in us. To know ourselves, we must know what our fears are.

Few of us would claim to be utterly free from the fear of death, for example. If the caregiver has followed a similar life-style or participated in the same risk behaviors as the one with AIDS, then the death fears may be very direct and conscious. You may see in that wasting disease what you might become in the future. Then the anxiety arises: given the increasing decimation that AIDS is bringing, and the exhaustion of many present caregivers, will there be anyone left to care for me?

Regardless of the caregiver's own life-style, when death seems so evident around us, when its reality is close to so many friends, there are depressing effects. It is not just the loss of people we love, as important as that is. It is also the terrifying reminder of our own vulnerability and mortality. Fears will always affect our decisions—especially if we do not acknowledge them and deal with them.

Doubtless we have sexual fears, also. Though AIDS is a human, viral disease that anyone can contract, the larger numbers of those affected have been so through sexual contact. Although the epidemiological picture is changing, the greater numbers of those affected are still gay and bisexual men. So when you and I confront AIDS, at present at least, we must confront directly our feelings and, possibly, our fears about homosexuality. In a homophobic society, no one is immune from internalized homophobia—including gays and lesbians themselves. The dynamics of homophobia, as explored earlier in this book, are well borne in mind.

With AIDS, sexuality and death seem terribly closely connected. It is confusing because we are accustomed to experiencing them as quite different realities. We often use our sexuality as a defense *against* death fears. Sometimes we just escape our mortality through sex. Some of us unconsciously lean on procreation as a defense against death, finding assurance of our own immortality because we can pass life on to our children and grandchildren. However, homosexual people (even though many have parented children) symbolize nonprocreation, and nonprocreating people have always made a lot of other folks anxious. Think of the barren woman in ancient Israel, cursed because she bore no children. Think of how in early New England the childless woman was persecuted as a witch. Now, with the current epidemic, gayness brings mortality anxieties in a double way: it symbolizes nonprocreation, and it seems linked with a fatal disease.

Whenever we live as though death were the final word, we cultivate a life-style of death, indeed, a "death-style." Personally, we might then as well live for number one, and eat, drink, and be merry, "for tomorrow we die." Socially, we might as well build more bombs, at the cost of untold billions needed elsewhere. It is a death-style that distances us from and punishes everyone who reminds us too vividly that we too are mortal. A death-style is always deficient in compassion, for it makes us resent those who unmask our own vulnerabilities.

Fears that are acknowledged, shared, talked about, examined, and tested out against one's worldview may not completely vanish. Yet they do seem to lose some of their demonic powers. "Know thyself, and know thy fears." And our ethics will be the better for it.

Finally, our ethics are shaped by *the ways we name the implications of the disease we are facing.* Recall the power of the metaphorical naming of diseases. All of that holds true for the ways we name each of our connections with AIDS. It is no accident that most of those who have the disease passionately reject the term "victims of AIDS," strongly preferring "persons with AIDS." Likewise, most reject the description "dying with AIDS," insisting instead on "living with AIDS." Such language is serious business. For many it is quite literally a matter of the quality of one's survival, a matter of life instead of death while one still lives. What of that man who said, "At first I saw it only as a curse; now I see it as a blessing"?

I do not hear this as sentimentalizing a vicious disease. I am simply awed by how some persons with AIDS have named their realities in ways that have empowered them even in the midst of increasing physical debilitation. Yes, there is a difference between a victim and a person. There is a difference between dying and living until you die. The power of language, of naming our realities, is serious business. Caregivers and all others do well to listen carefully. We will learn more deeply that how we respond to any moral situation is profoundly shaped by the ways we interpret and name that situation.

The Healing of the Blind Man

What, then, does this awful disease mean? How can we fit this dreadful disease into our own meaning patterns? For the person of faith the question finally becomes, What is God doing in the midst of all this?

A good clue comes from the Gospel According to John. The story begins, "As he [Jesus] walked along, he saw a man blind from birth. His disciples asked him, 'Rabbi, who sinned, this man or his parents, that he was born blind?' " (John 9:1–2). Now that is a good question to raise if one is really into works righteousness, into using religion to make oneself feel good by feeling superior to others. But Jesus sweeps it aside, saying, "Neither this man nor his parents sinned; he was born blind so that God's works might be revealed in him" (v. 3).

Then Jesus, moved by compassion, assists in the man's healing by applying mud to his eyes and telling him to wash it off in the Pool of Siloam. The man comes back with his sight restored. Remember, all this occurs on the Sabbath. Once again—by healing on the Sabbath, a forbidden activity—Jesus has offended the pieties of the Pharisees and the righteousness of the religious law in order to reveal the power of the gospel.

Thus, the first thing in interpreting AIDS is to answer everyone who asks the self-serving, works-righteous question about punishment. God does not use disease to punish any more than God uses droughts or earthquakes to punish. Jesus made it plain that God simply does not govern the world by our moral judgments about who is righteous and who is not. God's ways are not the ways of fearful people. The Holy One sends both sun and rain on the just and the unjust, and the Gracious One's judgments of people are different from ours. That is a biblical response to every fearful, misguided identification of the AIDS epidemic as God's vengeance on the homosexual community. (Curiously, when some use this argument against all homosexually oriented persons they forget that, with regard to AIDS, lesbians are probably the safest of all groups.)

The story urges that we ask the right question. It is not the question of blame. It is the question of meaning: What works of God are possibly being revealed through this pain? What can we see of God's own suffering with those who suffer? What can we make of the energy and caring that we see all around us in this epidemic? How can we interpret the profound priesthood of AIDS caregivers? Are these not evidences of the divine energy and caring? What of the power of The Quilt, that massive fabric stitched by thousands, who put into cloth their celebration of particular lives and their common grief? Is this not God's celebration and grieving too?

Another point of the story is that we cannot let fear overcome us, for fear always limits our compassion. Jesus had reason to fear the wrath of the Pharisees (they regularly gave it to him!), for he broke their religious rules by healing on the Sabbath. In other instances, he readily touched and embraced persons whom others feared to touch—menstruating women, social outcasts, and even those afflicted with the dreaded leprosy.

If, as scripture says, "perfect love casts out fear," the opposite is also true: fear always casts out love and compassion. We simply cannot be compassionate to those whom we deeply fear. So, in the midst of this epidemic, God is teaching us to confront our own fears, specifically about sexuality and death, because AIDS has raised both of those fears so acutely for us and has packaged them right together. Doubtless there will continue to be some sincerely held biblical and theological differences in the church about issues of sexual orientation. Yet one thing is clear: fear casts out compassion, and as a church of Jesus Christ we cannot be both compassionate and fearful. Fear, revulsion, and condemnation cannot be justified by any biblical interpretation, no matter how sincerely such interpretation is held.

Hospitality to the stranger is a central theme of the biblical way of life. Throughout its history, the church in its finest moments has been a "social pioneer"—pioneering new ways of hospitality that the wider society was not yet ready to undertake. We can again be that social pioneer, creating islands of hospitality in an often fearful world.

Here is one small example. Several years ago a memorial service was held in the church to which I belong, a service for a man who died of AIDS. It was for Bill, one partner of the couple who had brought us the bran muffins and brownies, as I related in chapter 6. Because of so much religious rejection, Bill and his partner, Bob, had long been outside the church, indeed, ever since they became partners fourteen years earlier. Still, Bob wanted Bill's service to be held in a church sanctuary, because that would symbolize something of the faith they had never lost. That itself seemed a miracle—their faith's perseverance in the midst of an inhospitable religious climate. The service was held in our United Church of Christ congregation, which both men had been pleased to learn was an "Open and Affirming Church"—a denominational label for a congregation that has formally and publicly declared itself open to and affirming of persons without regard to sexual orientation.

When Bob came to make arrangements about using the building, our minister met him for the first time and said, "I hope that you'll feel at home here." As an openly gay man, Bob had never before heard those words in a church or from a minister. *I hope you'll feel at home here.* They were simple words, but they were healing words. The service was a healing event, attended by many who themselves had lost partners, friends, and sons of their own to AIDS. We might yet dare to believe that the church can be a house of prayer for *all* people.

PART FOUR

SERMONIC
CONCLUSIONS

12

I Thank God for You:
A Sermon for Lesbian and Gay
Awareness Week at United
Theological Seminary

In reflecting about this chapel service for Lesbian and Gay Awareness Week at United Seminary, I went back to the opening words of a number of Paul's letters. Listen to some of them: From his first letter to the Corinthians:

> I give thanks to my God always for you because of the grace of God that has been given you in Christ Jesus, for in every way you have been enriched in [God], in speech and knowledge of every kind—just as the testimony of [or *to*] Christ has been strengthened among you.
>
> (1 Cor. 1:4–6)

From his letter to the Philippians:

> I thank my God every time I remember you, constantly praying with joy in every one of my prayers for all of you, because of your sharing in the gospel from the first day until now.
>
> (Phil. 1:3–5)

From his first letter to the Thessalonians:

We always give thanks to God for all of you and mention you in our prayers, constantly remembering before our God . . . your work of faith and labor of love and steadfastness of hope in our Lord Jesus Christ.

(1 Thess. 1:2–3)

And from the second letter to the Thessalonians (perhaps not written by Paul himself, but surely in his spirit):

We must always give thanks to God for you, brothers and sisters, as is right, because your faith is growing abundantly, and the love of everyone of you for one another is increasing. Therefore we ourselves boast of you among the churches of God for your steadfastness and faith during all your persecutions and the afflictions that you are enduring.

(2 Thess. 1:3–4)

Additional thanksgivings from the apostle might be read, but these are sufficient. Now, I sometimes argue with Paul, as I imagine you do. I simply do not believe that some of his specific moral judgments (particularly about sexuality issues) stand the test of the very gospel that he proclaimed with such power. But that argument is for another day. Today I am caught up in his thanksgivings.

In fact, I was tempted to write a letter myself to some sisters and brothers in the faith. And I have done so. This letter will not get into anyone's scriptural canon. Please bear with me while I share this letter with you, especially with those of you who are gay and lesbian:

To my lesbian sisters and gay brothers in the faith: Grace and peace!

First, I thank God for you because you have been teaching me "a hermeneutic of suspicion." For far too long I was largely uncritical of my own assumptions in doing theology, but you have been teaching me a more healthfully suspicious theology. You have taught me, for example, to distrust sincerity as a validating criterion for theology. I used to think that when some Christians found homosexuality contrary to God's will on biblical grounds, their sincere use of the scriptures should be respected, even if I disagreed with their conclusions. I have come to believe that this is like saying that when white folks sincerely ground in the Bible their convictions that persons of color are inferior, we ought to respect their sincerity. Sincerity and elaborate uses of scripture are no guarantee of freedom from homophobia. We are, all of us, afflicted with that disease. You have taught me to be more creatively suspicious in doing theology.

Also, I thank God for you because you have made me more critically aware of our Christian tradition. For example, in pressing the question of blessing your unions you have made me more aware of our frequent errors in understanding the Christian tradition of marriage. So many of us have thought that clergy actually perform marriages, and that churches have a special power to create a valid marriage. It is not so. I am sure I have been guilty of sloppy language and thinking in the past, saying, for example, "I married Jane and John last Saturday night." (If I really meant what I said, that would have been an interesting *ménage à trois!*) But it is not so. Some of you have reminded me that only the covenant of two persons with each other and with God creates a union. The church has the opportunity to bless, celebrate, and support a union. But it is the covenanting process that creates a marriage, not the church or the clergy or a wedding service or a license. That applies to your unions just as much as it does to those of heterosexual people.

In refusing to bless your unions, most churches have used a double standard. For over three centuries most Protestants and increasingly many Roman Catholics have recognized that procreation is not the central criterion for sexuality and marriage. Love is. So the church's dominant majority has abandoned the centrality of the procreative norm. That is, we have abandoned it for heterosexual persons, but we have continued to apply it to you, insisting that your unions are not fit to recognize and celebrate because they will not be biologically procreative. You are calling us to look again at the tradition, with more critical faithfulness and single-standard integrity.

The church has condemned homosexual promiscuity. But when, in your own deep desire for and commitment to fidelity in intimacy, you have asked for the blessing of your unions, then churches have turned their backs on your covenants, branding them as unfit to celebrate. You are calling the rest of us on our deplorable moral hypocrisy. Yes, you are teaching me, and a lot of us, to be more honestly and critically faithful to the tradition.

Further, I give thanks for you because you have helped me, sometimes painfully, to recognize my sin. Years ago, some of your gay brothers and lesbian sisters first uncovered and challenged my pitiful and ugly homophobia. You, through them, put me on the road—a lifelong journey, I realize—to being a "recovering homophobic."

- You taught me how deeply connected were my homophobia and my male sexism.
- You taught me how much homophobia in men (and in me) is the projection of an anxious quest for masculinity.
- You taught me that I did not need to fear my desires for emotional intimacy and physical touch with other men, and that my life could be immeasurably enriched when that fear was diminished.
- Indeed, you have taught me to fear myself less and love myself more, and I thank God for you.

Further, I thank God because you have taught me much about our desperate need for more erotic spiritualities and theologies. Eros is that love born of our hungers and our need for one another. It is love with warmth and passion. The straight-white-male tradition has used the standard of agape, self-giving love, and has judged eros deficient, banishing it from Christian spirituality, to our impoverishment. So we have been made hostage by an agape reductionism. We have been captives of theologies that have cheapened, devalued, even vilified the erotic and confused it with the pornographic. We have been prisoners of beliefs in which the hunger, desire, passion, and yearning for fulfillment have been banished as inappropriate to Christian spirituality. I was reared on such theology.

But you have helped me to embrace a larger vision of divine and human loving. Dante found eros in the Love that moves the sun and the other stars, and many of you have also. I have come to see the divine eros as that fundamental energy of the universe that is the passion for connection and hence the hunger for justice and the yearning for life-giving communion.

How have you helped me to learn this? By your steadfast

refusal to divorce your sexuality from your spirituality. In the face of oppressive attempts to deny you your eros, you have refused to give up your passion for life-giving connection. You have helped me to learn, because you know so well that eros is the enemy of every dualism, every hierarchy, every oppression, and every joyless piety. You know so well that eros is the nurturer of celebration, of the passion for justice, and of empowerment for every daughter and son of God. I am grateful to have learned this from you, and I thank you.

I thank God for you, because you have helped me to embrace a more incarnational spirituality. Christians have long been called the people of the incarnation. But so often we have been embarrassed by God's embodiment and our own. By doctrine we have confined incarnation to one figure, Jesus, two millennia ago. In so doing we have denied his promise to us and to all others that we too might be God-bearing body-people. But, you have helped me to see that if we do not know the gospel in our bodies, we do not know the gospel. You have helped me to recognize that when we find bodily life an embarrassment to a so-called high-minded, spiritual religion, we lose feeling for the holiness of our own bodies. Then it is very difficult to feel the holiness of hungry bodies in our cities and the holiness of bodies ripped by torture in Central America.

You have helped me to know, as Teilhard de Chardin also taught us, that our bodies are not part of the universe that we possess totally—they are the totality of the universe that we possess partially.

I thank God for you because you have shown me a bigger church than I once knew. In *quantitative* size, you are a statistical minority. But in *qualitative* size, you are no minority. You are large and making the church larger.

You have had many reasons and many occasions to vote with your feet and leave the church. Yet you have stayed, because you believe that the gospel is for everyone. Yet many of you have stayed, because you still believe that the gospel is for all people. You have stayed because you still bear the hope that the church might yet be larger in stature—larger in the size of its soul, bigger in its integrity, greater in its ability to entertain a rich variety of persons, fuller in its strength of spirit to enable all people to realize their destiny to freedom, uniqueness, and worth. I thank God for your showing me the vision of a bigger church.

I thank God for you because you have been sacred clowns. You have placed a mask on the Communion table in this chapel as a symbol for this week. You have told us all that it is the grim reminder of the masks that others of us have often forced you to wear. It is also the joyful reminder of your having taken them off. That is a powerful image. And the mask also reminds me of the clown.

There is an ancient Christian tradition of the sacred clown—indeed, Christ as a clown. The mask reminded me of that. And it reminded me of the native American tradition of honoring the *heyoehkah,* sometimes called the *berdache.* The *heyoehkahs* were also sacred clowns, honored in the tribe for their important and special functions. They were those in the tribe who did things differently, who challenged people's thinking and shook them up, who kept them from becoming rigid. They were also called "contraries," because they did some things backward. They walked backward, danced backward, and did things contrary to what others considered normal. And the *heyoehkahs* were gay.

I thank God that you have shown us all a *heyoehkah* response to AIDS. When the so-called "normal" response was fear and panic, you sacred clowns danced backward and responded with love and compassion. When the world was talking about dying with AIDS, you were helping people to *live* with AIDS. When the "normal" response was to isolate, you sacred clowns did things "backward" and drew people into community. When most people said that this AIDS business is not about us, but about "them," you sacred clowns said, "This is about us all; our whole planet is sick and has acquired an immune dysfunction." I thank you for dancing the dance of the sacred clowns who do things differently.

Finally, sisters and brothers, in my deep thanksgiving for and celebration of you, I do not intend to put you on an unwanted pedestal. I assume that we are all sinners. H. L. Mencken once described the Puritan as the one who deep down had a nagging sense that some people, somewhere, might be enjoying themselves. Well, I have a nagging sense that all of us are sinners. All of us are broken and need healing, including you whom I particularly celebrate in this letter. But our sin does not lie in our sexuality or in our particular sexual orientations, whatever they may be. It is in our estrangement from love. But there, too, you have been my teachers, teaching me much about the meanings of love. And what is love?

Let our sister Carter Heyward, a marvelous lesbian theologian, say it for us. Hear her words:

> To say I love you is to say that you are not mine, but rather your own.
> To love you is to advocate your rights, your space, your self, and to struggle with you, rather than against you, in our learning to claim our power in the world. . . .
> To love you is to be pushed by a power/God both terrifying and comforting, to touch and be touched by you. To love you is to sing with you, cry with you, pray with you, and act with you to re-create the world.
> To say "I love you" means—*let the revolution begin!*[1]

Yes, I thank God for you. Grace and peace, and God bless the revolution! Amen.

I3

Who Is Christ for Us Today?
A Holy Week Sermon
at United Theological Seminary

Once when Jesus was praying alone, with only the disciples near
him, he asked them, "Who do the crowds say that I am?" They
answered, "John the Baptist; but others, Elijah; and still others,
that one of the ancient prophets has arisen." He said to them,
"But who do you say that I am?"

(Luke 9:18–20a)

Quite aware of what might be waiting for him on his last trip
to Jerusalem, Jesus asked his disciples, "Who do the crowds say
that I am?" The disciples gave him a variety of answers: "Some
say this . . . some say that . . . and still others say . . ." Then Jesus
pressed them. "But who do you say that I am?"

In this seminary we study Christology. "Who do the crowds of
theologians say that I am?" And we answer, "The Council of
Chalcedon says . . . Calvin says . . . Schleiermacher says . . .
Ruether says . . . Sobrino says . . . " Yet, the Christ will not let us
go. "But who do you say that I am?"

Dietrich Bonhoeffer, awaiting his execution at the hands of
the Nazis, wrote from his prison cell, "Who is Christ for our

day?" The words are important. Not simply "Who is Christ?" but "Who is Christ *for our day?*" Now the question is both inescapably personal and contemporary. And, "How can we reclaim for Christ a world which has come of age?"[1]

In retrospect, I realize that I have met many Christs. I first met Christ at my mother's knee as the gentle Jesus, meek and mild. He seemed to me, as best I can recall, some combination of a clean, smiling baby in the manger, Sallman's *Head of Christ* in sepia tones, and perhaps a bit of the Easter bunny—all mixed together. I liked that warm and friendly Christ. Gradually that Christ disappeared as my childish sentimentality faded. But even now, years later, something of that warmth remains.

Growing into adolescence, I met Christ as the ideal of religious purity and moral perfection. Here was the model for the Presbyterian youth group, where my attendance was an enforced ritual. But here, also, was one who left me feeling guilty. I did not measure up. That Christ's purity was asexual, but as an adolescent my hormones were in high gear. The holiness of that Christ was a religious perfection, but I constantly felt rebelliously irreligious. That Christ seemed unreal and oppressive. That image too began to fade. Yet something of that Christ's challenge to my integrity and wholeness is still very real.

In college I met a Christ who was both theologically incomprehensible and unbelievable. I could not fathom the formulas of Nicaea and Chalcedon, the miraculous union of one who was fully God and fully human. Though I could not then articulate it, I knew that the dualistic assumptions lying behind such formulas were not good news for me, but bad news. I could not believe that there was an infinite gulf between divinity and humanity, a gulf bridged only once, leaving the rest of us fated with our deficient humanity and needing rescue by a supernatural Savior. I fled from that Christ, and from all things Christianly orthodox. Yet there remains a sense of Christ's unfathomable mystery that will not let me go.

Sometime in my twenties, I met Christ the healer. Years earlier I had dismissed the miraculous New Testament healings as quaint remainders of a first-century worldview. The healing of the blind and disabled, the raising of Lazarus—these were fanciful things a young modern could not believe. But through a study of Paul's letter to the Romans, my eyes were opened in new ways. I realized that I too was blind and disabled, hungering for a healing, gracious God. In Christ I had now heard a rumor of grace. I am still strongly drawn to that rumor of grace.

It was some years later that I began meeting a prophetic, liberating Christ. I first met that one in the 1960s embodied in courageous Mississippi blacks, in whose modest homes there always hung a picture of Jesus. I met that one in the 1970s in the peaceful anger of war protesters commanding my country to put away its swords. A decade later I saw that one in the faces of amazingly hopeful Nicaraguans who knew that American-financed contras could not finally destroy those for whom Christ was liberator. I met that gender-transcending Christ in women pronouncing a clear and firm "No" to patriarchy and holding up a vision of a different world than I had known. I met that Christ in gay men and lesbians who could have voted with their feet, but who stayed in the church because they believed that the gospel is for all people. That liberating Christ remains strong and pointing to the future.

Something of each of these Christs is still with me, something even from the childhood and youthful images. But there is one more Christ I must name—one who is increasingly important to me. That is the Christ of the empty tomb.

The event occurred in a garden. "Early on the first day of the week, while it was still dark, Mary Magdalene came to the tomb and saw that the stone had been removed from the tomb." Weeping, she said, "They have taken away my Lord, and I do not know where they have laid him." Then one whom she had mistaken for the gardener said to her, "Mary!" But when she recognized him, he said, "Do not hold on to me." (John 20:1–17, selected.) Or, as other translations have it, "Do not cling to me" (John 20:17, NEB and JB). Go to my brothers and sisters—the power of God is in the world, and in you.

So the tomb is empty. Christ is alive. Christ is not confined in Jesus of Nazareth, or in the first century, or in the sixteenth, or in any doctrinal theories. I dare not cling too closely to Christ as a past event, lest I miss the incarnation present now. It is now or never, for the now is all we have.

Where is God's embodiment now? Where does Word become flesh? Walt Whitman wrote:

Why should I wish to see God better than this day?
I see something of God each hour of the twenty-four,
    and each moment then,
In the faces of men and women I see God, and in my own face
    in the glass.[2]

Come then, to still another garden, a garden of lovers. Listen
to words from the Song of Solomon. The woman speaks:

> Arise, my love, my fair one,
>   and come away; for now the winter is past,
>   the rain is over and gone.
> The flowers appear on the earth;
>   the time of singing has come,
> and the voice of the turtledove
>   is heard in our land.
>   (S. of Sol. 2:10–12)

And the man speaks:

> How fair and pleasant you are,
>   O loved one, delectable maiden!
> . . . .
> Oh, may your breasts be like clusters of the vine,
> . . . .
> and your kisses like the best wine.
>   (S. of Sol. 7:6–9)

Can this too be a picture of the christic presence today? To be
sure, the Song depicts an almost idyllic picture. It looks like
sexuality without the fallenness of that other garden, Eden. No
fig leaves needed here. No bodily shame. In this garden there is
no sexism, no dominance or submission. The woman is fully the
equal of the man. Each honors the worth and beauty of the other,
and together they embrace their sexuality without hint of guilt or
exploitation. The lovers delight not only in each other but also in
the sensuous delights of the natural world around them—
flowers, fruits, fountains.

Here, surely, is God's gift of the erotic. Here is love with
passion and heart, love that is warm and moist, love that
searches for fulfillment in both giving and receiving. Here is our
hunger to taste and smell, to see and touch. Here is the flow of
our senses, the sacred power of our desire. Without all of this,

love as sacrifice and self-giving becomes cold. Without this, the world itself becomes hard and metallic.

Can God's own love be erotic? Not a dispassionate, self-sufficient deity dispensing divine favor to helpless humans, but the Lover yearning, seeking, desiring? Can that be true? "In the beginning was the Word" (John 1:1). When that Word came to dwell with us, it became no abstract doctrine, no sacred book, no code of morality. It became flesh.

Jesus, to the horror of squeamish Christians, was a laughing, crying, sweating, eating, drinking, digesting, urinating, defecating, sexual, sensuous bundle of flesh just as we are. If we cannot believe that, we shall have difficulty believing in the holiness of our own bodies. If we cannot believe that, we shall have difficulty believing that we have met God in one of us—and still meet God in flesh. But there is the good news! God embraces human flesh as the fitting vehicle of divine presence. God's embodiment continues wherever our love becomes flesh and our flesh becomes love. The divine dwells among us full of grace and truth. The tomb is empty. Matter is blessed. Incarnation is still real. Might we still "behold that glory"?

In a culture that does not really honor matter but cheapens it, in a culture that does not love the body but uses it, belief in God's incarnation is countercultural stuff. We will need some death and resurrection. Yet those realities are not foreign to our faith.

Do you remember that resurrection scene in Thornton Wilder's homely, wise play *Our Town*? Through the miracle of the playwright, Emily Gibbs, who had died in childbirth in her mid-twenties, is allowed to leave her grave on the hill above Grover's Corners and return to life for one day. Against the counsel of others in the graveyard who tell her that the return will be too painful, she decides to come back for one day, and chooses her twelfth birthday.[3]

The scene of her return opens in the kitchen, where her mother is busy fixing breakfast. Fourteen years have gone by. Emily pleads with Mama to look at her, just for a moment, as though she really saw her. Mama, however, is too busy.

This is the way the day unfolds. People are too busy to notice or to touch. Before long it is too much for her, and Emily cries out that she can't go on. It is too painful. It goes too fast. She never realized all that was going on, and people never noticed. She pleads to be taken back up the hill to her grave. But first she takes one more look and says her goodbyes.

How sensual and bodily are her farewells! The divine yearning for the incarnational mystery is there. Emily says goodbye to the world, and to Grover's Corners, and to Mama and Papa. She bids farewell to clocks that are ticking and to Mama's sunflowers. She says goodbye to food and coffee and newly ironed dresses, to hot baths and sleeping and waking. She exclaims that the earth is just too wonderful for anyone to realize it. Does anyone, she wonders, ever realize life while they are living it? Or are we blind to it all? A moment later the Stage Manager suggests to her that perhaps saints and poets do, at least sometimes.

Who is Christ for us today? And where do we meet the christic presence? No single answer will be adequate. But perhaps the empty tomb might have its place among our answers. Then, in the midst of an often painful, unjust, and terror-filled world, we might also find Christ as the erotic presence of the Cosmic Lover who still meets us in the flesh of our days: the One who promises that the winter shall be past, the flowers shall appear on the earth, the time of singing shall come, and the voice of the turtledove shall be heard in our land.

Amen.

Notes

Chapter 1. Sexuality and Spirituality: Agenda for a Continuing Revolution

1. Robert Bellah et al., *Habits of the Heart: Individualism and Commitment in American Life* (New York: Harper & Row, 1985).

2. Carter Heyward, *Touching Our Strength: The Erotic as Power and the Love of God* (San Francisco: Harper & Row, 1989).

3. Sallie McFague, *Models of God* (Philadelphia: Fortress Press, 1987), 126.

4. On the problems of the church's definition of and practices about "the family," see Janet Fishburn, *Confronting the Idolatry of the Family* (Nashville: Abingdon Press, 1991).

5. Charles E. Curran, "Roman Catholic Sexual Ethics: A Dissenting View," in *Sexual Ethics and the Church: After the Revolution* (Chicago: Christian Century Foundation, 1989), 51.

6. Robert McAfee Brown, *Spirituality and Liberation: Overcoming the Great Fallacy* (Philadelphia: Westminster Press, 1988), 104f.

Chapter 2. Where Are We? Seven Sinful Problems and Seven Virtuous Possibilities

1. See also James B. Nelson, "Religious Dimensions of Sexual Health," in *Readings in Primary Prevention of Psychopathology: Basic Concepts,* ed. Justin M. Joffe et al. (Hanover, N.H.: University Press of New England, 1984).

2. See Joanne Carlson Brown and Carole R. Bohn, eds., *Christianity, Patriarchy and Abuse: A Feminist Critique* (New York: Pilgrim Press, 1989).

3. Helpful documentations of these teachings of the church fathers can be found in Frank Bottomley, *Attitudes to the Body in Western*

Christendom (London: Lepus Books, 1979), chs. 4–6; and in Raymond J. Lawrence, Jr., *The Poisoning of Eros* (New York: Augustine Moore Press, 1989), ch. 3.

4. John Milton, *Paradise Lost,* ed. Scott Elledge (New York: W.W. Norton & Co., 1975), Book IV, 91.

5. Evgenii Lampert, *The Divine Realm* (London: Faber & Faber, 1944), 97f.

6. See John D'Emilio and Estelle B. Freedman, *Intimate Matters: A History of Sexuality in America* (New York: Harper & Row, 1988), ch. 10.

Chapter 3. Doing Body Theology

1. See Don Johnson, *Body* (Boston: Beacon Press, 1983), esp. ch. 3.

2. See Kenneth J. Shapiro, *Bodily Reflective Modes: A Phenomenological Method for Psychology* (Durham, N.C.: Duke University Press, 1985).

3. See Seymour Fisher, *Body Experience in Fantasy and Behavior* (New York: Appleton-Century-Crofts, 1970); *Body Consciousness* (Englewood Cliffs, N.J.: Prentice-Hall, 1973); *Development and Structure of the Body Image,* vol. 2 (Hillsdale, N.J.: Lawrence Erlbaum Assocs., 1986). Fisher says, "Although we are still in the early stages of understanding body image phenomena, we have discovered that body attitudes are woven into practically every aspect of behavior. The full range of their involvement cannot be overstated" (*Development and Structure,* 625). There is reason to assume that our bodyself experiences as females and as males are more similar than dissimilar. Here I am dealing in the basic human commonalities of body experience. Nevertheless, there are also certain important differences of world perception related to our different sexual biologies as well as to our sex-role conditioning. I have described some of these with their possible theological-ethical implications in *The Intimate Connection: Male Sexuality, Masculine Spirituality* (Philadelphia: Westminster Press, 1988).

4. Brian Wren, *Bring Many Names* (Carol Stream, Ill.: Hope Publishing Co., 1989). I wish to record my genuine gratitude to Brian Wren for dedicating this hymn to me.

5. Kenneth J. Gergen, "The Social Constructionist Movement in Modern Psychology," *American Psychologist* 40:266–275. Social constructionism is indebted to a number of different intellectual schools, such as symbolic interactionism, literary deconstructionism, symbolic anthropology, existentialism, phenomenology, and, in general, to social psychological theory. It may be contrasted with empiricism and

positivism, which stress the objectively definable reality of topics of investigation. Cf. Peter L. Berger and Thomas Luckmann, *The Social Construction of Reality* (Garden City, N.Y.: Doubleday & Co., 1966).

6. See Herbert Blumer, *Symbolic Interactionism: Perspective and Method* (Englewood Cliffs, N.J.: Prentice-Hall, 1969).

7. See Michael Foucault, *The History of Sexuality*, vol. 1: *An Introduction* (New York: Pantheon Books, 1978). While others (Peter J. Naus, Jonathan Weeks, Kenneth Plummer, William Simon, and John Gagon) have also pursued a largely social constructionist or symbolic interactionist position, and while they too argue against the notion that the body is universal in its sexual drives and expressions, this still remains a minority position among sexual scholars. For my own application of this approach, see James B. Nelson, *Embodiment: An Approach to Sexuality and Christian Theology* (Minneapolis: Augsburg Publishing House, 1978), esp. ch. 1. Social constructionist feminists are well represented by Carter Heyward's *Touching Our Strength,* esp. ch. 2.

8. See H. Richard Niebuhr, *Radical Monotheism and Western Culture* (New York: Harper & Brothers, 1960), 102ff.

9. In Frederick W. Turner III, ed., *The Portable North American Indian Reader* (New York: Viking Press, 1973), 253.

10. Wendell Berry, in Elizabeth Roberts and Elias Amidon, eds., *Earth Prayers* (New York: HarperCollins, 1991), 306.

11. Pierre Teilhard de Chardin, *Science and Christ* (New York: Harper & Row, 1968), 12f.

12. For a helpful and extended discussion of these problems, see Tom F. Driver, *Christ in a Changing World* (New York: Crossroad, 1982).

13. Two writers who have grasped this insight well are Charles Davis, *Body as Spirit: The Nature of Religious Feeling* (New York: Seabury Press, 1976), and Arthur A. Vogel, *Body Theology* (New York: Harper & Row, 1973).

14. Thomas Traherne, *Poems, Centuries and Three Thanksgivings,* ed. Anne Ridler, 174, 177, quoted in A. M. Alchin, *The World Is a Wedding: Explorations in Christian Spirituality* (New York: Crossroad, 1982), 41.

15. Toni Morrison, *Beloved* (New York: New American Library, 1987), 88.

Chapter 4. Sources for Body Theology: Homosexuality as a Test Case

1. Channing E. Phillips, "On Human Sexuality," May 5, 1985. Quotation taken from a photocopy of the sermon.

2. *New York Times,* May 26, 1985, sec. I, 39.

3. I was one of those called in for consultation, and I subsequently led the church retreat some months later. I mention this because I felt Riverside's events a bit from the inside and not entirely as an outside observer.

4. William Sloane Coffin, "The Fundamental Injunction: Love One Another," Sermons from Riverside, May 12, 1985 (duplicated), 1f.

5. Ibid., 3.

6. An excellent discussion of Wesley's quadrilateral can be found in Colin W. Williams, *John Wesley's Theology Today* (Nashville: Abingdon Press, 1960), ch. 2.

7. For more detail about the specific biblical texts that make direct references to certain forms of same-sex activity, see Nelson, *Embodiment,* ch. 3, n. 7, and ch. 8.

8. Robin Scroggs has formulated these questions succinctly in his important study *The New Testament and Homosexuality* (Philadelphia: Fortress Press, 1983), 123. The entire volume is a persuasive illustration of the application of these questions.

9. Ibid., 126.

10. Walter Wink, "Biblical Perspectives on Homosexuality," *The Christian Century,* Dec. 7, 1979, 1085.

11. L. William Countryman, *Dirt, Greed, and Sex* (Philadelphia: Fortress Press, 1988).

12. John Wesley, in John Telford, ed., *The Letters of John Wesley,* Standard Edition, vol. 5 (London: Epworth Press, 1931), 364. Commenting on 1 Corinthians 14:20, Wesley also said, "Knowing religion was not designed to destroy any of our natural faculties, but to exalt and improve them, our reason in particular." Cf. Williams, *John Wesley's Theology Today,* 30.

13. See Alfred C. Kinsey et al., *Sexual Behavior in the Human Male* (Philadelphia: W. B. Saunders, 1948). See also his *Sexual Behavior in the Human Female* (Philadelphia: W. B. Saunders, 1953).

14. George Weinberg, a psychotherapist, is usually credited with popularizing the term. See his *Society and the Healthy Homosexual* (Garden City, N.Y.: Doubleday & Co., Anchor Press, 1972), ch. 1.

15. For a fuller discussion of the dynamics of homophobia, see Nelson, *The Intimate Connection,* ch. 3, n. 3, and 59ff.

16. For a review of literature on the subject of this chapter, see my article "Homosexuality and the Church: A Bibliographical Essay," *Prism* 6, no. 1 (Spring 1991):74–83.

Chapter 5. Men and Body Life: Aging as a Case Study

1. Victor J. Seidler, *Rediscovering Masculinity: Reason, Language and Sexuality* (London: Routledge & Kegan Paul, 1989), 7.

2. Archibald MacLeish, "The Wild Old Wicked Man," *Collected Poems, 1917–1982* (Boston: Houghton Mifflin Co., 1985), 492f.

3. See Barbara P. Payne, "Sex and the Elderly: No Laughing Matter in Religion," *Quarterly Papers on Religion and Aging 5*, no. 4 (Summer 1989).

4. Susan Sontag, "The Double Standard of Aging," *Saturday Review of the Society 55*, no. 39 (Oct. 1972), 29ff.

5. See General Assembly Special Committee on Human Sexuality, *Keeping Body and Soul Together: Sexuality, Spirituality, and Social Justice* (Louisville, Ky.: Presbyterian Church (U.S.A), 1991), 114ff.

6. See William H. Masters, Virginia E. Johnson, and Robert C. Kolodny, *Human Sexuality*, 4th ed. (New York: HarperCollins, 1992), 258ff.; Gordon S. Walbroehl, M.D., "Effects of Medical Problems on Sexuality in the Elderly," *Medical Aspects of Human Sexuality 22*, no. 10 (Oct. 1988), 56f.

7. See Raymond M. Berger, *Gay and Gray: The Older Homosexual Man* (Urbana, Ill.: University of Illinois Press, 1982), 193ff.

8. David J. Maitland, *Aging as Counterculture: A Vocation for the Later Years* (Cleveland: Pilgrim Press, 1991).

9. Carl J. Jung, *Modern Man in Search of a Soul* (New York: Harcourt, Brace & Co., 1933), 108. See also Maitland, *Aging as Counterculture*, 68ff. and 93ff.

10. See Nancy Datan and Dean Rodeheaver, "Beyond Generativity: Toward a Sensuality of Later Life," in *Sexuality in the Later Years*, ed. Ruth B. Weg (New York: Academic Press, 1983), 286f.

11. Christopher Fry, *The Lady's Not for Burning* (New York: Oxford University Press, 1950), 88.

12. See Beverly Wildung Harrison, *Making the Connections* (Boston: Beacon Press, 1985), 162ff. Also Janet Fishburn, *Confronting the Idolatry of the Family* (Nashville: Abingdon Press, 1991).

13. See Harrison, *Making the Connections*, 157ff.

14. Dag Hammarskjöld, *Markings*, trans. Leif Sjöberg and W. H. Auden (New York: Alfred A. Knopf, 1970), 89.

Chapter 6. Revelation in Men's Experience: "I Need—I Hurt—I Can't"

1. James Weldon Johnson, "The Creation," in *God's Trombones: Seven Negro Sermons in Verse* (New York: Viking Press, 1927), 17.

2. See John Carmody, *Toward a Male Spirituality* (Mystic, Conn.: Twenty-third Publications, 1990), 90.

3. Alan Alda, "What Every Woman Should Know About Men," in *Men's Lives*, ed. Michael S. Kimmel and Michael A. Messner (New York: Macmillan Publishing Co., 1989), 294ff.

4. Alan Wolfelt, "Gender Roles and Grief: Why Men's Grief Is Naturally Complicated," *Thanatos*, Fall 1990, 23.

5. See Samuel Osherson, *Finding Our Fathers: The Unfinished Business of Manhood* (New York: Free Press, 1986).

6. See Brown and Bohn, *Christianity, Patriarchy and Abuse*, ch. 2, n. 2.

7. See also Nelson, *The Intimate Connection*, ch. 3, n. 3; ch. 5.

8. Dietrich Bonhoeffer, *Prisoner for God: Letters and Papers from Prison*, ed. Eberhard Bethge, trans. Reginald H. Fuller (New York: Macmillan Co., 1953), 124.

9. Ibid., 164. While removing Bonhoeffer's masculine pronouns for God in this quotation, I have left his masculine references for humanity as a reminder that this speaks with particular force to our male experience.

10. See Bernard Loomer, "S-I-Z-E," *Criterion* 13, no. 3 (Spring 1974), and "Two Kinds of Power," *Criterion* 15, no. 1 (Winter 1976).

11. Bonhoeffer, *Prisoner for God*, 131.

12. *Good News for Modern Man* is the American Bible Society's title for its contemporary translation of the New Testament. While the title ought to be gender-inclusive, my play with those words intends the male reference.

Chapter 7. Men as Pastors and Counselors: Manly Pitfalls and Possibilities

1. See Charles V. Gerkin, *The Living Human Document: Revisioning Pastoral Counseling in a Hermeneutical Mode* (Nashville: Abingdon Press, 1984), 27.

2. The Diagram Group, *Man's Body: An Owner's Manual* (New York: Paddington Press, 1976).

3. James E. Dittes, *The Male Predicament* (New York: Harper & Row, 1985), 164f.

4. Gerkin, *Living Human Document*, 26f.

5. For a good summary of this movement, see Don S. Browning, *Religious Thought and the Modern Psychologies* (Philadelphia: Fortress Press, 1987), 61–93; also, Browning, "The Pastoral Counselor as Ethicist: What Difference Do We Make?" *The Journal of Pastoral Care* 42, no. 4 (Winter 1988), 294.

6. See Don S. Browning, *The Moral Context of Pastoral Care* (Philadelphia: Westminster Press, 1976).

7. Edward W. L. Smith, *The Body in Psychotherapy* (Jefferson, N.C.: McFarland & Co., 1985), 3.

8. Quoted in Smith, *The Body in Psychotherapy*, 3.

9. Boston Women's Health Book Collective, *Our Bodies, Ourselves* (New York: Simon & Schuster, 1973), 3, italics mine.

10. Some of the illustrative material that follows has been used in a different and more expanded form in Nelson, *The Intimate Connection*, ch. 3, n. 3.

11. Daniel C. Maguire, "A Catholic Theologian at an Abortion Clinic," *MS.* 13, no. 6 (Dec. 1984), 132.

12. Martin Buber, *I and Thou,* trans. Walter Kaufman (New York: Charles Scribner's Sons, 1970), 69. Carter Heyward's work puts Buber's relational theology into a radically incarnational Christian interpretation. See esp. her *The Redemption of God* (Washington, D.C.: University Press of America, 1982); and " 'In the Beginning Is the Relation': Toward a Christian Ethic of Sexuality," *Integrity Forum* 7, no. 2 (Lent 1981).

13. See James W. Prescott, "Body Pleasure and the Origins of Violence," *The Futurist* 9, no. 2 (1975).

14. Beverly Wildung Harrison expresses these things well in "Human Sexuality and Mutuality," in *Christian Feminism,* ed. Judith L. Weidman (New York: Harper & Row, 1984), 147ff.

Chapter 8. Medical Care and the Meanings of Bodily Life

1. Ann Davidson, "Modified Radical," *The New England Journal of Medicine* 321, no. 9 (Aug. 31, 1989), 639.

2. Eric J. Cassel, M.D., "The Nature of Suffering and the Goals of Medicine," *The New England Journal of Medicine* 306, no. 11 (Mar. 18, 1982), 639f.

3. Ibid., 640.

4. See Jacques Sarano, *The Meaning of the Body,* trans. James H. Farley (Philadelphia: Westminster Press, 1966), 54, 72ff.

5. Stan Nevins, "The Challenge of Embodiment: A Philosophical Approach," *Journal of Humanistic Psychology* 19, no. 2 (Spring 1979), 29ff.

6. See Stanley Hauerwas, "Salvation and Health: Why Medicine Needs the Church," in *Theology and Bioethics,* ed. Earl E. Shelp (Dordrecht, Boston, Lancaster and Tokyo: D. Reidel, 1985), 216ff.

7. See Nevins, "The Challenge of Embodiment," 31.

8. See Harmon L. Smith and Larry R. Churchill, *Professional Ethics and Primary Care Medicine* (Durham, N.C.: Duke University Press, 1986), to whom I am indebted for insights in this section.

9. H. Tristam Engelhardt, Jr., "The Social Meanings of Illness," *Second Opinion* 1 (1986), 29.

10. See Suzanne Poirier and Daniel J. Brauner, "Ethics and the Daily Language of Medical Discourse," *Hastings Center Report* 18, no. 4 (Aug.–Sept. 1988), 5ff.

11. Ibid., 6.

12. See Cassel, "The Nature of Suffering," 641.

13. Sarano, *The Meaning of the Body*, 96.

14. See Smith and Churchill, *Professional Ethics and Primary Care Medicine*, esp. 59–67.

15. Ibid., 66.

16. See Sarano, *The Meaning of the Body*, 78.

17. Hauerwas, "Salvation and Health," 223.

18. Audre Lorde, *The Cancer Journals* (Argyle, N.Y.: Spinsters Ink, 1980), 77.

Chapter 10. Embryos and Ethics: Old and New Quandaries About Life's Beginnings

1. The Congregation for the Doctrine of the Faith, "Instructions on Respect for Human Life in Its Origin and on the Dignity of Procreation: Replies to Certain Questions of the Day," Feb. 22, 1987, as reprinted in the *New York Times*, Feb. 23, 1987.

2. Ibid.

3. Richard A. McCormick, "Therapy or Tampering? The Ethics of Reproductive Technology," *America* 153, no. 17 (Dec. 7, 1985).

4. Since the publication of *Human Medicine: Revised and Expanded Edition* (Minneapolis: Augsburg Publishing House, 1984), my position on this issue has shifted to a somewhat less restrictive one. While I still believe that some legal safeguards against exploitation are warranted, I am now more concerned about the restrictions on women's bodily self-determination. See *Human Medicine*, 106.

Chapter 11. Illness as Body Interpretation: HIV and AIDS

1. See Susan Sontag, *Illness as Metaphor* (New York: Farrar, Straus & Giroux, 1978).

2. See Judith Wilson Ross, "An Ethics of Compassion, a Language of Division: Working Out the AIDS Metaphors," in *AIDS: Principles, Practices, and Politics,* ed. Inge B. Corless and Mary Pittman-Lindeman (Washington, D.C.: Hemisphere Pub-

lishing Corporation, 1988), esp. 83–86. See also David G. Hallman, ed., *AIDS Issues: Confronting the Challenge* (New York: Pilgrim Press, 1989).

3. See Susan Sontag, *AIDS and Its Metaphors* (New York: Farrar, Straus & Giroux, 1989), to whom I am indebted for many insights here.

4. See Kent L. Sandstrom, "Confronting Deadly Disease: The Drama of Identity Construction and Management Among Gay Men with AIDS-Related Infections," *The Life Course Center Working Papers Number 89-4* (Minneapolis: Department of Sociology, University of Minnesota, 1989), whose excellent empirical study informs the paragraphs to follow.

5. Victor Turner develops the notion of liminality in *The Ritual Process* (Ithaca, N.Y.: Cornell University Press, 1969).

6. See Sandstrom's applications of liminality to AIDS, *Working Papers*, 9.

7. Sandstrom, *Working Papers*, 29. For an illuminating account of the process of embracing a different disease, see Audre Lorde, *The Cancer Journals*.

8. Brian Coyle, *Coming to Terms: The Coyle Journals* (Minneapolis: Equal Time, 1991), 5.

9. The American Medical Association survey, published in the *Journal of the American Medical Association,* was reported in the (Minneapolis) *Star-Tribune,* Nov. 27, 1991. The survey also stated that 50 percent of the doctors surveyed said they would not work with AIDS patients if given a choice and that 26 percent said that dying patients made them uneasy.

10. Role and relationship issues are well addressed in Leonard I. Pearlin, Shirley J. Semple, and Heather Turner, "The Stress of AIDS Care Giving: A Preliminary Overview of the Issues," in *AIDS: Principles, Practices, and Politics,* 279–290.

Chapter 12. I Thank God for You: A Sermon for Lesbian and Gay Awareness Week at United Theological Seminary

1. Carter Heyward, *Our Passion for Justice* (New York: Pilgrim Press, 1984), 93.

Chapter 13. Who Is Christ for Us Today? A Holy Week Sermon at United Theological Seminary

1. Dietrich Bonhoeffer, *Prisoner for God: Letters and Papers from Prison,* 157.

2. Walt Whitman, "Song of Myself," *Walt Whitman's Leaves of*

Grass, ed. Malcolm Cowley (New York: Penguin Books, 1959), sec. 48, p. 83.

3. See Thornton Wilder, *Our Town,* Harper Colophon edition (New York: Harper & Row, 1964), 99–100.

Acknowledgments

Grateful acknowledgment is given for permission to reprint the following copyrighted material.

Excerpt from "Prayers and Sayings of the Mad Farmer," from *Farming: A Handbook,* copyright © 1969 by Wendell Berry. Reprinted by permission of Harcourt Brace Jovanovich, Inc.

"Modified Radical," by Ann Davidson, first appeared in *The New England Journal of Medicine* 321, no. 9 (Aug. 31, 1989), 639f. Used by permission of *The New England Journal of Medicine.*

Excerpt from *Markings,* by Dag Hammarskjöld, trans. W. H. Auden/ L. Sjöberg. Translation copyright © 1964 by Alfred A. Knopf, Inc., and Faber & Faber, Ltd. Reprinted by permission of Alfred A. Knopf, Inc., and Faber & Faber, Ltd.

Excerpt from *Our Passion for Justice,* by Carter Heyward, copyright © 1984 by The Pilgrim Press. Reprinted by permission of The Pilgrim Press.

"The Creation," from *God's Trombones,* by James Weldon Johnson, copyright 1927 The Viking Press, Inc., © renewed 1955 by Grace Nail Johnson. Used by permission of Viking Penguin, a division of Penguin Books USA Inc.

Index